THE EMMA GEES

Bouchard

THE EMMA GEES

By

HERBERT W. McBRIDE

Captain, U. S. A.
Late Twenty-first Canadian Battalion

Illustrated
with Photographs and
Trench Maps

Lancer Militaria
Mt. Ida, Arkansas

Lancer Militaria reprint edition, 2003

Originally published by
Bobbs-Merrill, 1918

New Material ©1988, 2003 by Lancer Militaria

Printed in the United States of America

ISBN 0-935856-14-5

Lancer Militaria
PO Box 1188
Mount Ida, AR 71957
USA

In Flanders' fields the crosses stand—
Strange harvest for a fertile land!
Where once the wheat and barley grew,
With scarlet poppies running through.
This year the poppies bloom to greet
Not oats nor barley nor white wheat,
But only crosses, row by row,
Where stalwart reapers used to go.

Harvest in Flanders—LOUISE DRISCOLL

INTRODUCTION

When the final history of this war is written, it is doubtful if any other name will so appeal to the Canadian as Ypres and the Ypres Salient; every foot of which is hallowed ground to French, Belgians, British and Colonials alike; not a yard of which has not been consecrated to the cause of human liberty and baptized in the blood of democracy.

Here the tattered remnants of that glorious "contemptible little army," in October, 1914, checked the first great onrush of the vandal hordes and saved the channel ports, the loss of which would have been far more serious than the capture of Paris and might, conceivably, have proved the decisive factor in bringing about a Prussian victory in the war.

Here the first Canadian troops to fight on the soil of Europe, the Princess Pat's, received their trial by fire and came through it with untarnished name, and here, also, the First Canadian Contingent withstood the terrible ordeal of poison gas in April, 1915, and, outnumbered four to one, with flank exposed and without any artillery support worthy of mention, hurled back, time after time, the flower of the Prussian army, and, in the words of the Commanding General of all the British troops: "saved the situation."

Here, too, as was fitting, we received our baptism of fire (Second Canadian Division), as did also the third when it came over.

For more than a year this salient was the home of the Canadian soldier and Langemarck, St. Julien, Hill 60, St. Eloi, Hooge, and a host of other names in this sector, have been emblazoned, in letters of fire, on his escutcheon.

Baffled in his attempts to capture the city of Ypres, the Hun began systematically to destroy it, turning his heaviest guns on the two most prominent structures: The Halles (Cloth Hall), and St. Martin's Cathedral, two of the grandest architectural monuments in Europe. Now there was no military significance in this; it was simply an exhibition of unbridled rage and savagery. With Rheims Cathedral, and hundreds of lesser churches and châteaux, these ruins will be perpetual monuments to the wanton ruthlessness of German kultur.

When we first went there the towers of both these structures were still standing and formed landmarks that could be seen for miles. Gradually, under the continued bombardment, they melted away until, when I last passed through the martyred city, nothing but small bits of shattered wall could be seen, rising but a few feet above the surrounding piles of broken stones.

Glorious Ypres! Probably never again will you become the city of more than two hundred thousand, whose "Red-coated Burghers" won the day at Courtrai, against the trained army of the Count d'Artois; possibly never again achieve the commercial prominence enjoyed but four short years since; but your name will be forever remembered in the hearts of men from all the far ends of the earth where liberty and justice prevail.

H. W. McB.

NEW NAMES FOR OLD LETTERS

When reading messages sent by any "visual" method of signaling, such as flags, heliograph or lamp, it is necessary for the receiver to keep his eyes steadily fixed upon the sender, probably using binoculars or telescope, which makes it difficult, if not impossible, for him to write down each letter as it comes, and as this is absolutely required in military work, where nearly everything is in code or cipher, the services of a second man are needed to write down the letters as the first calls them off.

As many letters of the alphabet have sounds more or less similar, such as "S" and "F," "M" and "N" and "D" and "T," many mistakes have occurred. Therefore, the ingenuity of the signaler was called upon to invent names for certain of the letters most commonly confused. Below is a list of the ones which are now officially recognized:

A pronounced ack
B   "   beer
D   "   don
M   "   emma
P   "   pip
S   "   esses
T   "   tock
V   "   vick
Z   "   zed

The last is, of course, the usual pronunciation of this letter in England and Canada, but, as it may be unfamiliar to some readers, I have included it.

After a short time all soldiers get the habit of using these designations in ordinary conversation. For instance, one will say: "I am going over to 'esses-pip seven,'" meaning "Supporting 'Point No. 7," or, in stating the time for any event, "ack-emma" is A. M. and "pip-emma" P. M.

As the first ten letters of the alphabet are also used to represent numerals in certain methods of signaling, some peculiar combinations occur, as, for instance: "N-ack-beer" meaning trench "N-12," or "O-don" for "O-4."

"Ack-pip-emma" is the Assistant Provost Marshal, whom everybody hates, while just "pip-emma" is the Paymaster, who is always welcome.

Thus, the Machine Gunner is an "Emma Gee" throughout the army.

CONTENTS

LIST OF ILLUSTRATIONS

LIST OF ILLUSTRATIONS—*Continued*

THE EMMA GEES

THE EMMA GEES

CHAPTER I

HEADED FOR THE KAISER

THE following somewhat disjointed narrative, written at the solicitation of numerous friends, follows the general course of my experience as a member of the Machine Gun Section of the Twenty-first Canadian Infantry Battalion. Compiled from letters written from the front, supplemented by notes and maps and an occasional short dissertation covering some phase of present-day warfare and its weapons and methods, it is offered in the hope that, despite its utter lack of literary merit, it may prove of interest to those who are about to engage in the "great adventure" or who have relatives and friends "over there." The only virtue claimed for the story is that it is all literally true: every place, name and date being authentic. The maps shown are exact reproductions of front-line trench maps made from airplane photographs. They have never before been published in this country.

I am sorry I can not truthfully say that the early reports of German atrocities, or the news of Belgium's wanton invasion impelled me to fly to Canada to enlist and offer my life in the cause of humanity.

No, it was simply that I wanted to find out what a "regular war" was like. It looked as though there was going to be a good scrap on and I didn't want to miss it. I had been a conscientious student of the "war-game" for a good many years and was anxious to get some real first-hand information. I got what I was looking for, all right.

The preliminaries can be briefly summarized. The battalion mobilized at Kingston, Ontario, October 19th, 1914, and spent the winter training at that place. The training was of the general character established by long custom but included more target practise and more and longer route marches than usual. The two things we really learned were how to march and how to shoot, both of which accomplishments stood us in good stead at a later date.

Leaving Kingston May 5th, 1915, we sailed from Montreal the following morning on the *Metagama*, a splendid ship of about twelve thousand tons. We had as company on board, several hospital units, including about one hundred and fifty Nursing Sisters, all togged up in their natty blue uniforms and wearing the two stars of First "Leftenant," which rank they hold. And, believe me, they deserve it, too. Of course they were immediately nicknamed the "Bluebirds." Many's the man in that crowd who has since had cause to bless those same bluebirds in the hospitals of France and England.

We ran into ice at the mouth of the St. Lawrence and for two days were constantly in sight of bergs. It was a beautiful spectacle but I'm afraid we did not properly appreciate it. We remembered the *Titanic*.

Then we got word by wireless that the *Lusitania* had been torpedoed. I think an effort was made to suppress this news but it soon ran throughout the ship. Personally, I did not believe it. I had had plenty of experience of "soldier stories," which start from nowhere and amount to nothing, and besides, I could not believe that any nation that laid any claims to civilization would permit or commit such an outrage. I began to believe it however when, next day, we received orders to go down in the hold and get out all our guns and mount them on deck. We had six guns; two more than the usual allotment for a battalion; two having been presented to our Commanding Officer, Lieutenant-Colonel (now Brigadier-General) W. St. Pierre Hughes, by old associates in Canada, just a few days before our departure.

Two of the guns were mounted on the forward deck, two on the flying bridge and two on the aft bridge. I'm not sure, to this day, just what we expected to do against a submarine with those machine guns, but at any rate they seemed to give an additional feeling of security to the others on board and of course we machine gunners put up an awful bluff to persuade them that we could sink any U-boat without the least difficulty. Of one

thing we were sure. Being a troop ship we could
expect no mercy from an enemy and we were at
least prepared to make it hot for any of them who
came fooling around within range provided they
came to the surface. I was with the forward guns
and, as we had several days of pretty rough
weather, it was a wet job. Our wireless was continually cracking and sputtering so I suppose the
skipper was getting his sailing orders from the
Admiralty as we changed direction several times
a day. We had no convoying war-ships and sight-
ed but few boats, mostly Norwegian sailing vessels, until, one night about nine o'clock, several
dark slim shadows came slipping up out of the
blackness and established themselves in front, on
both flanks and behind us. We gunners had been
warned by the captain to look out for something
of the kind, but I can assure any one who has not
been through the experience that the sigh of relief which went up from those gun crews was sin-
cere and deep. We were running without lights,
of course, and none but the crew was allowed on
deck. The destroyers (for such they were), were

also perfectly dark and we could barely discern their outlines as they glided silently along, accommodating their pace to ours.

Just before sunrise we dropped anchor inside Plymouth breakwater. This was a surprise, as we had expected to land at Liverpool or Bristol. But you may depend on it, no one made any complaint; any port in England looked good to us. A few hours later we moved into the harbor and tied up at Devonport Dock where we lay all day, unloading cargo. Right next to us was a big transport just about to sail for the Dardanelles. The Dublin Fusiliers were aboard her and they gave us a cheer as we came in. Poor devils, they had a rough time of it down there; but I guess by this time they think the same about us; so we'll call it square.

It rained all day, but we finally got everything off the ship and on the trains and pulled out about dark. No one knew where we were going. The only training camp we had heard of in England was Salisbury Plain and what we had heard of that place did not make any of us anxious to see it. The First Canadian Division had been there and the reports they sent home were anything but encouraging. Our men were nearly all native-born Canadians and "Yankees," and they cracked many a joke about the little English "carriages," but they soon learned to respect the pulling power of the engines. We made ourselves as comfortable as possible with eight in a compartment, each man with his full kit, and soon after daylight the train stopped and we were told to get out. The name of the station was Westerhanger but that did not tell us anything. The native Britishers we had in our crowd were mostly from "north of the Tweed" so what could they be expected to know about Kent. For Kent it was, sure enough, and after a march of some two or three miles we found ourselves "at home" in West Sandling Camp. And how proudly we marched up the long hill and past the Brigade Headquarters, our pipers skirling their heartiest and the drummers beating as never before. For we were on exhibition and we knew it. The roads were lined with soldiers and they cheered and cheered as we came

marching in. We were tired, our loads were
heavy and the mud was deep, but never a man in
that column would have traded his place for the
most luxurious comforts at home.

There came a time when we hated that hill and
that camp as the devil hates holy water, but that
Sunday morning, marching into a British camp,
with British soldiers, eager to keep right on across
the channel and clean up Kaiser Bill and feeling as though we were able to do it, single-handed—why, the meanest private in the Twenty-first
Canadians considered himself just a little bit better
than any one else on earth.

Thus we came to our home in England, where
we worked and sweated and swore for four solid
months before we were considered fit to take our
place in the firing-line. All that time, from the
top of Tolsford Hill, just at the edge of our camp,
we could see France, "the promised land"; we
could hear the big guns nearly every night, and we,
in our ignorance, could not understand why we
were not allowed to go over and settle the whole
business. We marched all over Southern Eng-

land. I *know* I have slept under every hedge-row in Kent. We dug trenches one day and filled them up the next. We made bombs and learned to throw them. We mastered every kind of signaling from semaphore to wireless, and we nearly wore out the old Roman stone roads hiking all the way from Hythe to Canterbury. We carried those old Colt guns and heavy tripods far enough to have taken us to Bagdad and back.

But, oh, man! what a tough lot of soldiers it made of us. Without just that seasoning we would never have been able to make even the first two days' marches when we finally did go across. The weaklings fell by the wayside and were replaced until, when the "great day" came and we embarked for France, I verily believe that that battalion, and especially the "Emma Gees," was about the toughest lot of soldiers who ever went to war.

(Emma Gee is signaler's lingo for M. G., meaning machine gunner.)

It must not be inferred that our four months in England were all work and worry. Personally, I

9

derived great pleasure from them. We were right in the midst of a lot of old and interesting places which figure largely in the early history of England. Within a mile of our camp was Saltwood Castle, built in 499 by the Romans and enlarged by the Normans. It was here that the conspirators met to plan the assassination of Thomas à Becket at Canterbury, only sixteen miles away, and which we had ample opportunities to visit. Hythe, one of the ancient "Cinque Ports," was but a mile or so distant, with its old church dating from the time of Ethelbert, King of Kent. In its crypt are the bones of several hundred persons which have been there since the time of the Crusaders, and in the church, proper, are arms and armor of some of the old timers who went on those same Crusades. Among numerous tablets on the walls is one "To the memory of Captain Robert Furnis, Commanding H. M. S. Queen Charlotte: killed at the Battle of Lake Erie: 1813"—Perry's victory. About three miles away was "Monk's Horton, Horton Park and Horton Priory," the latter church dating from the

Photo by Western Newspaper Union

French Hotchkiss Gun Firing at Aeroplane

twelfth century and remaining just about as it was when it was built. Then there was Lympne Castle, another Roman stronghold; Cæsar's Plain and Cæsar's Camp, where Julius is said to have spent some time on his memorable expedition to England; and, within easy reach by bicycle, Hastings and Battle Abbey where William the Norman defeated Harold and conquered England. The very roads over which we marched were, many of them, built by the Romans. Every little town and hamlet through which we passed has a history running back for hundreds of years. We took our noon rest one day in the yard of the famous "Chequers Inn," on the road to Canterbury. We camped one night in Hatch Park, where the deer scampered about in great droves. On Sundays we could charter one of the big "rubber-neck" autos and make the round trip to Margate, Ramsgate, Broadstairs, Deal and Dover.

But, just the same, when we were told, positively, that we were going to leave, there were no tears shed. We had gone over there to fight and nothing else would satisfy us.

CHAPTER II

THE Machine Gun Section, having its own transport, traveled via Southampton, as there were better facilities for loading horses and wagons there than at the ports from which the remainder of the troops embarked. After we had everything aboard ship it was an even bet among the crowd as to whether we were going to France, the Dardanelles or Mesopotamia. There were other ships there, loading just as we were, some of which were known to be destined for the eastern theater; so how could we know? As a matter of fact, our officers did not know any more about it than the men.

On the dock I discovered a box containing blank post-cards given out by "The Missions to Seamen." I wrote one to my mother and stuck it in a mail-box, on the chance that it *might* go through. I had no stamps and didn't really expect it to be taken up, but some

12

one "with a heart" inscribed on it "O. H. M. S.," and, sure enough, On His Majesty's Service it went, straight to Indianapolis.

POST CARD. SOUTHAMPTON
PAID

SEP 14

Mrs. Ida S. McBride
1434 Park Ave
Indianapolis,
Indiana
U. S. A.

After having everything nicely stowed in the hold, Sandy McNab and I had to go down and dig out a couple of guns to mount on deck. It required quite a lot of acrobatic stunts to get down in the first place and then to get the guns and ammunition up, but we managed to finish the job just before dark and got the guns mounted, mine on the starboard and Sandy's on the port side, before we steamed out. It was a black drizzly

13

night and the cold wind cut like a knife, but we "stood to" until dawn, expecting anything or nothing. After an hour or so we didn't care much what happened.

Everything was dark, not a light showing aboard ship or elsewhere until, about midnight, I saw a glow on the horizon, nearly dead ahead. As the ship's lookouts said nothing, I did likewise, but I assure you I was mightily puzzled. I knew we could not be near enough to shore to see a lighthouse and, anyway, there was too much light for any ordinary shore signal. I finally concluded that it must be a ship burning and wondered what we would do about it, but the thing gradually took on the appearance of a gigantic Christmas tree and then I felt sure that I was going "plumb nutty." I sneaked over to McNab's side and found him in about the same frame of mind. We were both too proud to ask questions, so we simply stood there and watched—what do you suppose?—*a hospital ship!* lighted from water line to truck with hundreds of electric lights; strings of them running from mast-head to mast-

14

head and dozens along the sides, fitted with reflectors to throw the light down so as to show the broad green stripe which is prescribed by the Geneva Convention. Then we both laughed. Little did we think then that we would both be coming back to "Blighty" on just such a ship; Sandy within a few weeks and I more than a year later.

Before daylight we picked up a string of beacons, red and white, and dropped anchor. As soon as it was light we could see the harbor of Le Havre. I had been there before and recognized it quickly enough. Then we knew that France was our destination.

After waiting for the proper stage of the tide, the anchor was weighed, and with a lot of fussy little tugs buzzing about, now pushing at one end and then scurrying around to give a pull at the other, we finally tied up to the dock at our appointed place and prepared to disembark. The docks were thronged with men, mostly in some sort of uniform and all busy. Many of the French soldiers were wearing the old uniforms of blue and red, while others were clothed in corduroy. The new "horizon blue" had not yet been adopted. There were many English soldiers, mostly elderly men of the so-called "Navvie's Battalions," but among all the others, was quite a number whose uniform was the subject for much speculation until some one happened to notice that they were always working in groups and were, invariably, accompanied by a *poilu* carrying a rifle with bayonet fixed. It was our first sight of German prisoners and it gave us a genuine thrill. The war was coming closer to us every minute.

Disembarking was nothing more than common, every-day, hard labor, relieved, occasionally, by the antics of some of the horses that did not want to go down the steep narrow gangway. It was the devil's own job to get them aboard in the first place and equally difficult to persuade them to go ashore. Such perversity, I have noticed, is not confined to horses: the average soldier can give exhibitions of it that would shame the wildest mustang.

We had been living, since leaving Sandling, on "bully beef" and biscuits, but here on the dock we found one of those wonderful little coffee canteens, maintained and operated by one of the many thousands of noble English women who, from the beginning of the war, have managed, God knows how, always to be at the right place at the right time, to cheer the soldier on his way; working, apparently, night and day, to hand out a cup of hot coffee or tea or chocolate to any tired and dirty Tommy who happened to come along. If you have any money, you pay a penny; if you are broke, it doesn't make the least bit of difference; you get your coffee just the same, and the smile that always accompanies the service is as cheerful and genuine in the one case as in the other. Many women of the oldest and most aristocratic families of England have given, and are still giving, not only their money but their personal labor to this work; making sandwiches, boiling tea, yes, and washing the dishes, too, day after day and month after month. You do not often hear of them; they are too busy to advertise. But Tommy knows and I venture the assertion that no single sentence or "slogan" has been as often used among the soldiers in France as "God bless the women."

So we finally got everything off, wagons loaded and teams hitched up, and about mid-afternoon made our way through the quaint old city to a "rest camp" on the outskirts where we had time to wash and shave and eat another biscuit before we received orders that we were to march, at midnight, and entrain at Station No. —. It commenced to rain about this time and never let up until we had entrained the next morning.

That was a night of horrors. Sloshing through the mud, over unknown roads and streets, soaked to the skin. Oh! well, it was a very good initiation for what was to follow, all right, all right.

Polite language is not adequate to describe the loading of our train: getting all the wagons on the dinky little flat-cars and the horses aboard. The horses fared better than the men for, while they were only eight to a car, we were forty or more; and in the same kind of cars, too. They look like our ordinary cattle cars but are only about one-half as big. Forty men, with full equipment, have some difficulty to crowd into one, let alone to sit or lie down. And, of course, everything we had was soaked through. When I come to think of it, the strangest thing about the whole business was that there were no genuine complaints. The usual "grousing," of course, without which no soldier could remain healthy, but I never heard a word that could have been taken to indicate that any one was really unhappy. While we were loading, our cooks had managed to make up a good lot of hot tea and that helped some. We also got an issue of cheese and more bully and biscuits and, after filling up on these, everybody joined in a "sing-song" which continued for hours.

This subject of soldier's songs would make an interesting study for a psychologist. Not being versed in this science I can only note some of the peculiarities which impressed me from time to time.

The first thing that one notices is the fact that the so-called soldier's songs, written by our multitudinous army of "popular" song-smiths to catch the fleeting fancy of the patriotically aroused populace, are conspicuous by their absence. No matter how great a popularity they may achieve among the home-folk and even the embryo soldiers, during the early days of their training, they seldom survive long enough to become popular with the soldiers in the field. When in training, far away from the field of battle, soldiers appear very fond of all the "Go get the Kaiser" and "On to Berlin" stuff and are not at all averse to complimenting themselves on their heroism and invincibility, with specific declarations of what they are going to do. Sort of "Oh, what a brave boy I am," you know. But as they come closer to the real business of war, while their enthusiasm and determination may be not a whit less, they become more reserved and less prone to self-advertisements; so, as they *must* sing something, they fall back on the old-timers, such as *Annie Laurie* or *My Old Kentucky Home* when they feel particularly sentimental, and for marching songs, any nonsensical music-hall jingle with a "swing" to it will serve.

STRAIGHT TO THE FRONT

Our crowd was what might be called "a regular singing bunch" and had a large and varied repertoire, including everything from religious hymns to many of that class of peculiar soldier's songs which although vividly expressive and appropriate to the occasion are, unfortunately, not for publication. Among the most popular were *The Tulip and the Rose, Michigan* and *There's a Long, Long Trail Awinding,* together with several local compositions set to such airs as *John Brown's Body* and *British Grenadiers.* You might hear *Onward, Christian Soldier* sandwiched between some of the worst of the "bad ones" or *Calvary* followed by *The Buccaneers.* You never heard that last one, and never will, unless you "go for a soldier."

I've heard men singing doleful songs, such as *I Want to Go Home,* when everything was bright and cheerful with no sign of war, and I have heard them, in the midst of the most deadly combat, shouting one of Harry Lauder's favorites, as *I Love a Lassie.* I once saw a long line "going over the top" in the gray of the morning, and when they had got lined up, outside the wire, and started on their plodding journey which is the "charge" of now-a-days, one waved to his neighbor who happened to be on a slight ridge above him and sang out: "You tak the High Road an' I'll tak the Low Road." And immediately the song spread up and down the line; even above the tremendous roar of the guns you could hear that battalion going into action to the tune of *Loch Lomond*.

So, you see, there is a difference between "songs about soldiers" and "soldier's songs," the latter being the ones he sings because they appeal to his fancy and the former including the long and constantly growing list of cheaply-sentimental airs intended for home consumption. The difference between the two classes is as great as that between war as it really is and war as the people at home think it is. This is a difference which will never be understood by any excepting those who have been over there. Those so unfortunate as to be unable to learn it at first hand will be forever ignorant of the real meaning of war.

STRAIGHT TO THE FRONT

There is no language which can adequately describe it; no artist can paint it; no imagination can conceive it. It is just short of the knowledge of one who has died and returned to life. So, by all means, let us have songs if they serve to cheer or amuse any one, whether at home or abroad.

It will probably do the soldier no harm to have people think he is a "little tin god on wheels" any more than it will hurt him to be belittled by the sickly mollycoddling name of "Sammie," no matter how deeply he resents it. It is astonishing to me that our newspapers persist in the use of this appellation in the face of the fact, which they should know, that it is obnoxious to the American soldier himself. Would they call a Canadian or Australian or Scotch soldier a "Tommy"? If they do, I advise them to hide out and do it by telephone. Such sobriquets, to be of any real value, must come spontaneously; perhaps by accident; possibly conferred by an enemy. They can never be "invented."

But, to get back to our story. This country

through which we passed is an historical pageant,—from the very port of Harfleur, which figures largely in the stories of both Norman and English invasion, all the way up the valley of the Seine. Who could see Rouen, for the first time, without experiencing a thrill of sentiment as the memories of Jeanne d'Arc, Rollo the Norman, Duke William, Harold and many others come forth from their hiding-places in the back of one's brain? Although we passed through without a stop, we could see the wonderful cathedral and the hospice on the hill and, crossing the river, we had a fleeting glimpse of the delightful little village of St. Adrien, with its curious church, cut out of the face of the chalk cliff; where the maidens come to pray the good Saint Bonaventure to send them a husband within the year.

On, past the field of Crécy, across the Somme which was to us only a name at that time but to become "an experience" at a later date, we made our slow progress across northern France. At a certain junction we were joined by the rest of the battalion which had traveled from England by a different and shorter route.

24

STRAIGHT TO THE FRONT

In the early hours of the morning we came to our stopping place, St. Omer, which was then the headquarters of the British Expeditionary Force in France. We did not tarry, however, but before daylight were on the march—eastward. We stopped for a couple of hours, near some little town, long enough to make tea, and then went on again. This was the hardest day we had had. Every one was overloaded, as a new soldier always is, and, moreover, our packs and clothing had not dried and we were carrying forty or fifty pounds of water in addition to the regulation sixty-one-pound equipment. Then, too, the roads were of the kind called *pavé;* that is, paved with what we know as cobble-stones or Belgian blocks. On the smooth stone or macadamized roads of England we would not have minded it so much, but this kind of going was new to us: ankles were continually turning, our iron-shod soles eternally slipping on the knobbed surface of the cobbles and, take it all in all, I consider it the hardest march I have ever done, and I have made forty-eight miles in one day over the snow in the Northwest, too.

THE EMMA GEES

About dark we were halted at a farm and told that we were to go into bivouac and would probably remain there for a week or more. Now, one characteristic of the good machine gunner is that he is always about two jumps ahead of the other fellow, so, there being a big barn with lots of clean straw in it, we just naturally took possession while the rest of the troops were patiently waiting for the Quartermaster to assign them to billets. Of course we had a fight on our hands a little later but, by a compromise which let the signalers and scouts come in with us, we were enabled to hang on to the best part of the place. From names inscribed on the beams we learned that the Princess Pat's had once occupied the same place, and from the people who lived there we heard tales of how the Germans had carried off all their stock when they made their first great advance. All this was the next day, however, as we were too tired even to eat that night; we simply dropped on the straw and slept.

Next morning was bright and fair and everybody got busy, drying kits, overhauling and cleaning the guns and ammunition and fixing up our quarters for the promised week's rest. About four o'clock in the afternoon we were ordered to form up and march to a place about two miles distant, where, we were told, General Alderson, Commander-in-Chief of the Canadians, was to give us a little talk.

We arrived at the appointed place ahead of time, and while we were lying about waiting we had our first glimpse of real war. It was a long way off and high up in the air but it was a thrilling sight for us. A couple of German airplanes were being shelled by some of our anti-aircraft guns, and as we watched the numerous shell-bursts, apparently close to the planes, we expected, every moment, to see the flyers come tumbling down. However, none was hit and they went on their way. It was only later we learned that it is the rarest thing in the world for an airplane to be brought down by guns from the ground. I suppose I have seen several hundred thousand shots fired at them and have yet to see one hit by a shell from an "Archie" and only one by machine-gun fire from the ground. The majority of planes destroyed are shot down by machine guns in combat with other flyers.

When the General finally came, he looked us over and told us what a fine body of troops we appeared to be, and just for that, he was going to let us go right into the front line, instead of putting us through the usual preliminary stages in reserve and support. Of course we felt properly "swelled up" about it and considered it a great compliment. We did not know, what we now know, that they were about to start the big offensive which is known as the Battle of Loos and that the British had not enough troops in France to be able to afford such luxuries as reserves. It was a case of everybody get in and "get your feet wet."

As we were to march at daybreak, we had a busy night getting our scattered belongings together and repacked. This was our first experience of what shortly became a common occurrence and we soon learned that, in the field, a soldier never knows one day where he will be the next,

HÔTEL DU FAUCON.

CAFÉ-AÉRO

and thus he is always "expecting the unexpected."

We moved out at dawn and had another heartbreaking march as the weather had turned very warm. Through Hazebrouck and numerous small towns we continued our eastward way to Bailleul, stopping there for an hour's rest. Our section happened to be right in the market square so had a good opportunity to see some of the principal points of interest in this famous and ancient city. The Hotel de Ville with its curious weather-vane of twelfth-century vintage and the Hotel Fauçon particularly interested me: the former because I had read of it and the latter because it had real beer on ice. This is the place which Bairnsfather speaks of as the hotel at which one could live and go to war every day and I afterward did that very thing, for one day; leaving the frontline trenches in the morning, having a good dinner at the Fauçon and being back in the front line at night. That happened to be Thanksgiving Day; November 25, 1915.

After our rest we continued on our way and

29

arrived at the little town of Dranoutre, in Flanders, about five o'clock in the evening and went into bivouac. On this day's march we saw more evidence of war. Here and there a grave beside the road; occasionally a house that showed the effect of shell or rifle fire and, almost continually, firing at airplanes, both Allied and German.

At our camp we found detachments of the East Kents (The Buffs), and the Second East Surrey Regiment, from whom we were to take over a sector of the line. They said that it was comparatively quiet at that point but had been pretty rough a few months earlier.

The Machine Gun Section went in the next morning, two days ahead of the infantry, and the East Surreys remained during the two days to show us the ropes. They were a splendid lot of soldiers and I am sorry to say that when they left us it was to go to Loos, where they were badly cut up at the Hohenzollern redoubt. We never connected up with them again.

CHAPTER III

IN THE MIDST OF A BATTLE-FIELD

IT was a bright warm Sunday morning, that nineteenth day of September, when we made our first trip to the front-line trenches. Only the Number Ones, lance corporals, of each gun went in ahead, the guns and remainder of the section to come up after dark. I was a "lance-jack" at that time, in charge of No. 6 gun; and had a crew of the youngest boys in the section, two of whom were under seventeen when they enlisted and not one of whom was twenty at that time. Subsequent events proved them to be the equals of any in the whole section; a section of which a general officer afterward wrote: "I consider it the best in France." They were strong and healthy, keen observers, always ready for any duty and during all the time I was with them I never saw one of them weaken. They played the game right up to the finish, in fair weather and foul, during the easy times and the "rough," each until his appointed time came to "go West."

One, in particular, named Bouchard, a boy who enlisted when but sixteen, developed into the brightest and most efficient machine gunner I have ever known. His zeal and eagerness to learn so impressed me that it became my greatest pleasure to give him all the assistance in my power, and, despite the difference in our ages, there grew up between us such a friendship as can only be achieved between kindred spirits sharing the vicissitudes of war. Small of stature and slight of frame, it was only by sheer grit and determination that he was able to endure the terrible strain of that first winter. At times, when the mud was nearly waist deep, he would throw away his overcoat, blanket and other personal effects, but never would he give up his beloved gun. When trenches were absolutely impassable he would climb up on top, scorning bullets and shells, intent on the one job in hand—to get to his appointed station without delay. He was a constant source of inspiration to all of us, often inciting the older heads to undertake and achieve the apparently impossible by daring them to follow his lead.

Our sector was made up of what were then known as the "C" trenches, running north from the Neuve Eglise-Messines road and directly between Wulverghem and Messines. To the south of the road was the Douve River and just beyond that "Plugstreet" (Ploegstert). There had been some very hard fighting all along the Messines Ridge during the preceding year, but for several months things had been quiet. Now, by "quiet" I do not mean that there was any cessation of hostilities for there is always artillery firing and sniping going on, with a fair amount of rifle grenade and trench-mortar activity. It simply means that there is no attempt being made, by either side, to attack in force and to capture and hold captured ground.

Our route, that first morning, was rather a roundabout one, by way of Lindhoek, taken, as explained by our guide, because it was less exposed to enemy observation than a much shorter road which we used when moving at night. When

33

a short distance out from town, we passed in front of one of our howitzer batteries which decided that then was just the proper time to cut loose with a salvo, right over our heads. We were not more than fifty yards from the guns and the result was that we were all "scared stiff," to say nothing of being almost deafened. This appears to be a characteristic and never-ending joke with artillerymen and so we soon learned to "spot" their emplacements and go behind them, when possible.

At all cross-roads ("Kruisstraat," in Flemish), sentries were stationed who acted as guides and also gave warning of the approach of enemy aircraft. At a long blast of the whistle every person was supposed to stop and not make a move until the signal "all clear," indicated by two blasts, was given. It appears that, while the airmen have no difficulty in seeing moving objects on the ground it is next to impossible for them to locate stationary ones.

As we progressed, the signs of war were multiplied. Numerous graves along the road, each

34

Light Vickers Gun in Action Against Aircraft

marked by a cross, houses and barns torn by shells, a bridge and railroad track blown up and trees shattered and rent, until, finally, everything was desolation. When we arrived at Wulverghem, we had our first sight of a really "ruined" town. Of course we saw many worse ones later, but at that time, we could not conceive more complete destruction than had been wrought here by the German shells. Every building had been hit, perhaps several times; some had one or more walls standing, while many were totally destroyed and were nothing but piles of broken brick and mortar. Part of the church tower remained and one hand of the clock still hung to the side facing the German lines. This seemed to aggravate the boche as, every day, he would send from a dozen to forty or fifty shells over, all seemingly directed at the church tower.

As Messines Ridge is now "ours" I think there can be no objection to my going into details about our dispositions. Our Battalion Headquarters was located in the St. Quentin Cabaret, about two hundred yards south of Wulverghem and we

THE EMMA GEES

had a supporting gun, with infantry, at Souvenir
Farm and also at a redoubt near by, called "S-5."
Our front-line guns were distributed from the
Neuve Eglise road to the northern end of our
battalion frontage, about "C-3."

These numbers refer to certain locations on the
map, and the cabarets are not exactly such as one
is accustomed to seeing in American cities. They
are, or were, inns, such as in England would be
called public houses and in America, road houses.
In Flemish they are *herbergs,* but these happened
to bear French names, hence were called cabarets. One can not help wondering at the indis-
criminate manner in which French and Flemish
names are used in this corner of the world.
Neuve Eglise, Bailleul, Dranoutre and Locre are
all mixed up with Wolverghem, Ploegstert,
Wytschaete and Lindhoek: Ypres and Dickebusch
are neighbors; while St. Julian and Langemarck
lie side by side, as do Groot Vierstraat and La-
Clytte. Look at a map of West Flanders and the
adjoining parts of France and you will see what
I mean.

36

IN THE MIDST OF A BATTLE-FIELD

Just as we arrived at the Battalion Headquarters the signal was sounded, "German up,"
which is the short way of saying that an enemy
airplane is approaching, so we were obliged to
take cover and remain quiet for some time. We
were near a group of farm buildings and, going
inside, found that former occupants had left elaborate records of their visits. Among other mural
decorations were some rough sketches drawn by
Captain Bairnsfather, which afterward became
famous as "Fragments from France."

This suggests another interesting field for
speculation. Why is it that all men, regardless
of race, creed or color, have an inborn craving
to inscribe their names on walls and trees and
rocks, especially on walls other than those of
their own home? Wherever you go, all over the
world, you will find the carved or written record
stating that, at such and such a date, John Doe,
of Oskaloosa, Iowa, honored the place with his
presence. The buildings of Flanders and France
are storehouses of historical records. From
them the historian could almost reconstruct the

campaigns of the war. Would it not be an interesting task to make a thorough search of all the old buildings and dug-outs, just as the archeologists have been doing in Egypt and all the ancient habitations of mankind? The prehistoric caves of Spain or the cliff dwellings of the Colorado could not be more interesting than a compilation of these records, including the drawings and sketches, some of which are real works of art. Regimental crests and badges are often shown with the utmost attention to detail and, in one place which we afterward occupied, one of the walls bore an elaborately carved tablet enumerating the campaigns and battles of one of the oldest British line regiments, together with a list of the honors, V. C's. and so on, won by members thereof. On one of the walls at Captain's Post one of my boys, Charlie Wendt, carved a large maple leaf upon which he inscribed the names of all our squad. He was killed a few days later and others at various times and of that whole list, I am the sole survivor. I would give a great deal to have that bit of wall here in my own home.

IN THE MIDST OF A BATTLE-FIELD

Meantime, the *Allemand* has gone away and we are free to continue our journey to the front line.

In an orchard behind the house we entered a communication trench and after a few final words of advice from the guide as to the necessity of keeping our heads down wherever the walls were low, started on the mile-long trip. We learned that the trench by which we were going in was named Surrey Lane, in honor of the West Surreys who constructed it. At various points we came upon intersecting trenches, most of which were marked with the name of the point to which they led. One, I remember, was "Wipers Road"; not that it ran all the way to Ypres but led in the direction of that place.

Except for an occasional large shell, whispering overhead, consigned from Kemmel to Warneton or vice versa, and the distant muttering of the French guns away to the south, everything was quiet and peaceful, and had it not been for the ruined buildings and torn-up roads it would have been difficult to imagine that we were in the midst of a battle-field.

Passing through all the maze of cross trenches,

39

we finally reached the front line which we found to be what we afterward called a "half-and-half" trench; that is, it was dug down to a depth of perhaps four feet and built up about the same with sand-bags, making it possibly eight feet from the bottom of trench to top of parapet. It was quite dry and clean and comfortable and proved that the Buffs and Surreys had not been loafing during the summer. I'm afraid we did not properly appreciate it at that time, but as I look back over all the time that has passed since, I am compelled to admit that it was the finest bit of trench we ever occupied.

We had no more than arrived in the line than the cook of the first gun crew we struck brought out a "dixie" of tea and an unlimited supply of bread and butter and jam and invited us to fill up. ("Dixie" is the soldier's name for the camp kettle used in the British army.) Now if you have been paying attention to the story of our movements since leaving England, I think you can readily imagine that we were hungry. These soldiers had been out, some of them, **since**

the beginning of the war and had become inured
to all the hardships which are a necessary part of
the game, and, splendid fellows that they were,
the first thing they thought of was our comfort.
From that time on I never met up with any body
of British Imperial soldiers who did not show
this same consideration and solicitude for the
stranger. And they do it so unostentatiously and
naturally that they challenge the admiration of all,
especially of Colonials such as we, who were, I
fear, very apt to forget the little niceties of manner which are inbred in the native Briton. While
we afterward became the best of friends there
was never any danger of our becoming "alike."
We secretly admired their perfect and unalterable
observance of all orders even though we were, at
the same time, scheming to evade a lot of those
same restrictions which appeared to us to be unnecessary. They, on their part, could not help
admitting that the dash and "devil-may-care"
spirit shown by our men often accomplished results not otherwise attainable but from the emu-
lation of which they were barred by "traditions."

THE EMMA GEES

The discipline of the one and the discipline of the other are based on two entirely different modes of life; the former carefully trained to rely on and obey implicitly the orders of any superior officer, while the latter looks only for initial direction, depending upon his own initiative and ingenuity to see him through any trouble that might arise.

From this line we could see the whole valley which separated us from the famous Messines Ridge. The enemy was firmly established on its crest, with his advance lines in the valley and even, at some places, on the sides of the slope below us. The town of Messines, directly opposite, was in plain sight but nearly a mile away, the church and hospice, or infirmary, being conspicuous landmarks on the sky-line. Our front lines were from about one hundred and fifty to three hundred yards apart. Numerous ruined farms and cabarets were scattered along the line, sometimes in our territory and sometimes belonging to the enemy. These were, as a rule, con-

verted into redoubts or "strong-points," and de-
fended by both infantry and machine guns. To
the northward, within the German lines, was the
town of Wytschaete, while we had Mont Kemmel, a prominent hill which gave our artillery
good observation all the way from Ypres to
"Plugstreet."

Several of the prominent roads within the
German lines were in plain sight from our position and, while the artillery devoted considerable
attention to harassing the enemy, we were not
sufficiently supplied with ammunition at that time
to strafe them as was desirable. This was
especially true of several "dumps," which
is the colloquial word designating the
points where the wagons and motor transports deposit ammunition, food and other trench
stores and whence they are carried up to the front
line by the men. Thus an ammunition dump
means a point where ammunition is stored, while
a ration dump is a place where the ration carrying parties repair at night to procure the rations

43

for the following day. At some points the field cookers or "rolling kitchens" come up at night and the cooked food is carried from there to the front. One such place at Messines, we called "Cooker's Halt."

The machine gun officer of the outgoing Surreys had begun to develop some ideas of his own as to the feasibility of strafing enemy transports and dumps at night and had selected a tentative position behind a slight crest, about one hundred and fifty yards N. E. of "In den Kraatenberg Cabaret" and immediately adjacent to a disused communication trench called "Plum Avenue." Now I had been a crank on long range, indirect fire in England, so I had no difficulty in persuading our M. G. officer to turn this job over to me. We improved the position and also established another one, about one hundred yards down the trench for daylight work against aircraft. In those days the planes would come over at altitudes of two thousand feet and less and we had some splendid opportunities to practise on them. We succeeded in bringing one down with his petrol

44

French Using an Ordinary Wine Barrel on Which a Wagon Wheel Is Mounted to Facilitate the Revolving Movement to Any Desired Direction

tank on fire, and we turned back a good many more until they began to fly so high that we could not reach them. At night, by using information obtained from our artillery and our own forward observers, we were able to cut up a lot of their transports. At first they would drive down to a place called the Barricade, but after we caught them there two or three times they came only to the top of the hill, to "Cooker's Halt." We soon chased them out of that, however, and then I guess poor Fritz had to carry his stuff all the way from behind the Ridge. On two occasions we caught large working parties, in broad daylight, and cut them up and dispersed them. Our position in front of the group of buildings (In den Kraatenberg) naturally led the enemy to believe that we were using the building for cover, so he shelled the poor inoffensive houses and barns most industriously but never put anything close enough to our real position to do any damage. This taught me a lesson which I put into operation, later on, at Sniper's Barn, with the best of results.

45

THE EMMA GEES

From that time on, strafing was an important part of machine gunnery until, now, together with barrage fire, it comprises about all there is to machine-gun work, proper, for the automatic rifle has taken over the greater part of the front-line offensive work.

CHAPTER IV

Eight Days In

A S the subject of machine guns is one of great interest at this time, it may not be amiss to devote a little space to explaining some of the salient features of the most commonly used types.

All automatic arms are divided into classes, as determined by the following characteristics:

1st. Method of applying the power necessary to operate: (gas or recoil).

2nd. Method of supplying ammunition: (belt, magazine or clip).

3rd. Method of cooling: (water or air).

Another well-defined distinction is made between the true machine gun and the automatic rifle; the former being so heavy that it must be mounted on a substantial tripod or other base, while the latter is so light that it may be carried and operated by a single man. Of the former class, the Colt, (35 lbs.), the Vickers, (38 lbs.) and the Maxim, (63 lbs.) may be taken as representative. They are all mounted, for field work, on tripods weighing fifty pounds or more. In the latter class, the Lewis, Benet-Mercie, and Hotchkiss, running from 17 to 25 lbs., are fair examples. They are all equipped with light, skeleton "legs" or tripods, which, by the way, are never used in the field although they are still considered essential for training purposes.

In the gas-operated arms, a small hole is drilled in the under side of the barrel, six to eight inches from the muzzle, so that, when the bullet has passed this point, and during the time it takes it to traverse the remaining few inches to the muzzle, a certain portion of the enclosed gas is forced through this hole, where it is "trapped," in a small "gas-chamber" and its force directed against a piston or lever which, being connected with the necessary working parts of the gun by cams, links or ratchets, performs the functions of removing and ejecting the empty cartridge case, withdrawing a new cartridge from the belt, clip or magazine, and "cocking" the gun: that is, forcing the "hammer" or striker back and compressing its spring. As the pressure generated in the barrel by our ammunition is not less than 50,000 lbs. to the square inch, very little gas is required to do all this. There must also be sufficient force to compress or coil a strong spring or springs called "main-springs" or retracting springs which, in their turn, force the mechanism forward to its original position, seating the new cartridge in the chamber and releasing the striker, thus firing another shot. This action continues as long as the "trigger" is kept pressed or until the belt or magazine is emptied. The Colt, Benet-Mercie, Hotchkiss and Lewis are in this class. They are all of the air-cooled type.

In the recoil operated guns, the barrel itself is forced to the rear by the "kick," as we commonly call it, and the force applied directly to the working parts, thus performing the same operations above described. The Maxim, Vickers, Vickers-Maxim and Maxim-Nordenfeldt belong to this class. They are all water-cooled, having a water-jacket of sheet metal entirely surrounding the barrel.

All the last-mentioned class, and also the Colt, have the ammunition loaded in belts containing two hundred and fifty rounds each. The Hotchkiss and Benet-Mercie use clips of from twenty to thirty rounds, while the Lewis is fed from a round, flat, pan-shaped magazine holding forty-seven rounds. (For aircraft guns these magazines are made larger; about double this capacity, I think.)

During the early part of the war, before the advent of the Lewis and other automatic rifles, the only machine guns in general use were of the heavy, tripod-mounted type and it was necessary for them to advance with or even ahead of attacking troops. As the guns and tripods were very conspicuous objects they naturally became the especial targets for enemy riflemen and snipers and the casualties among machine gunners ran far above the average for other troops. It was this that caused the Emma Gee sections to be named Suicide Clubs.

Now, however, the Lewis gun, being light and inconspicuous, can be carried by advancing troops and used effectively in the attack without its operators suffering excessively, and at the same time it has been demonstrated that the true machine gun, of the heavier type, mounted on its firm base, can effectively cooperate with the artillery in maintaining protective or other barrages and in delivering harassing fire upon the enemy at points behind his front line. As this fire is, necessarily, over the heads of our own troops, sometimes but a few feet over them, it must be extremely accurate and dependable and it has been proved that guns of the lighter, automatic-rifle type, can not be safely used for this purpose, even when mounted on the heavy tripods of the other guns. This is probably due to the excessive vibration of the lighter barrels.

For the benefit of any who are not familiar with the word, I might say, in passing, that *"barrage"* is a French word meaning a "barrier" or a "dam" and when used in a military sense it means a veritable barrier or wall of fire, where the shells or bullets, or both, are falling so thickly as to make it impossible for any body of troops to go through without suffering great loss.

I know nothing of the Browning gun, as it is a new invention and has never been used in the field. We can only hope that it will prove as good as the Vickers and Lewis which are giving perfect satisfaction on the battle-fields of Flanders and France. No real machine gunner expects or requires anything better, but I can not imagine any *one* type of gun that can replace both of them any more than a single class of artillery can combine the functions of both the light field guns and the heavy howitzers.

The Germans evidently had good spies within our lines as they always knew when we changed over; that is, when we took over a new line. At first they would call out: "Hello, Canadians, how are you," sometimes even naming the battalion. Later on, however, they used much stronger language but they knew who we were, just the same. Their methods of communicating information from our lines were many and very ingenious.

For instance, at one time it was learned by our intelligence department that spies were making use of the many windmills to signal messages across the line. They did this by stopping the sails of the mills at certain angles and moving them about from time to time. When this was discovered the orders went out for all windmills to be stopped in such a position that the arms should always be at an exact forty-five degree angle whenever the mill was not running, with the understanding that failure to observe this regulation would result in our artillery in the immediate vicinity turning their guns on the offending mill. At one place we discovered a large periscope with a heliographic attachment by which a seemingly inoffensive Belgian peasant kept in constant communication with the boche. This periscope was concealed in the chimney of a partially ruined farm building within our lines. At other places underground cables were discovered, with telephones or field telegraph instruments concealed in cellars or old buildings. Carrier pigeons were also much used and, without a doubt, many men passed back and forth between the lines, some of them, as we learned from time to time, regularly enlisted in our armies. At several places we had men shot down and killed by snipers masquerading as farmers, behind our lines. Needless to say, such affairs were promptly attended to, on the spot, *"tout de suite,"* as the French say.

So, although that part of the line had been very quiet for a long time, they began at once to give us a reception. While the shelling was as nothing compared to bombardments we went through later, still it gave us an opportunity to make the acquaintance of the various kinds of shells from "whizz-bangs" up to something of about eight-inch caliber.

The first casualty in the battalion was a scout named Boyer who was killed on his initial trip into No Man's Land the first night in the trenches. Next day Starkey decided he could not see enough with a periscope, so took a look over the parapet. Both men are buried in the garden back of the St. Quentin Cabaret together with many from the best and most famous British Line Regiments.

The Emma Gees came out pretty lucky, having but one man seriously wounded. His name was Mangan, a Yankee, who had served in the U. S. Army in the Philippines. He was badly wounded by shrapnel and was sent back to England. We used to hear from him occasionally until about a year later the letters stopped.

After eight days we were relieved by the Twentieth Battalion and went back to Dranoutre for our first "rest." We went by way of Neuve Eglise but, as it was night, we could see but little of that much shot-up city. It commenced to rain before we started out and kept it up until we went back again, four days later. At that time it was customary to carry in and out everything, including ammunition, and we soon learned to dread the days when we had to move. We would have preferred to stay in the front line for a month at a time rather than carry all that heavy stuff in and out so often. However, we managed to get a bath and some clean clothes, which made everybody feel better. We had no regular billets at Dranoutre but rigged up little shelter tents, somewhat similar to those used in the U. S. Army, by lacing two or more rubber sheets together. Our cooking was done by gun crews, somewhat on the order of a lot of Boy Scouts, in that no two crews had the same ideas or used the same methods. My squad dug out a nice little "stove" in a bank, and by covering it with flattened-out biscuit tins and making a pipe of tin cans of various sorts, managed to get along very well. Here we received our first pay since arriving in France; fifteen francs each. It doesn't sound like much but, believe me, we made those "sous" go a long way and bought lots of little delicacies we could not otherwise have had.

While at Dranoutre we associated with the inhabitants, in the stores and estaminets. The Germans had taken of whatever they needed in the way of live stock and foodstuffs, but the town itself happened to be one of the many scattered up and down the line, which had miraculously escaped even an ordinary bombardment.

Quarter of a Franc
Present value about four cents

Half a Franc
Present value about eight cents

Quarter of a Franc
"Good for" about four cents

French Paper War-Money, Issued by the Various Municipalities.
Every Town Has its Bank of Issue. There are Practically no
Coins in Circulation

EIGHT DAYS IN

There were refugees, hundreds of them; from the towns and cities farther to the eastward, whence they had fled with little or nothing besides the clothes on their backs. There were children who had lost their parents; wives who knew not what had become of their husbands and men whose wives and families were somewhere back in the German-occupied territory. They told of enduring the direst hardships and suffering; of cold and hunger.

Every town behind the lines that had escaped destruction was crowded with these poor homeless people. Every habitable house sheltered all who could find no room to lie on the floor. Those who could, worked on the roads or in the neighboring fields. Many of the women worked in the military laundries. They all received some assistance from the French Government and from the many charitable societies. When talking with them they would tell their stories in a monotonous sort of way, seldom making any complaint; seeming to think that all these things were to be endured as a matter of course.

57

THE EMMA GEES

I have read all the available reports on the subject of atrocities and have no doubt that they are true, but none ever came under my personal observation.

In the midst of a battle many men do things which would, at other times, fill them with horror. The excitement of combat seems to breed a lust for killing and the sight of blood is like a red flag to a bull. This, unfortunately, is not confined to Germans. One of our officers who had had a brother killed a few days before deliberately shot and killed several unarmed prisoners. He was, himself, killed the same day. On another occasion, a wounded German, lying in a shell-hole, stabbed and killed one of our wounded and attacked another only to be beaten at his own game and killed with his own knife. A soldier of the Royal Fusiliers, at St. Eloi, was detected by his sergeant in the act of shooting an unarmed prisoner, whereupon the sergeant immediately shot and killed the soldier. I saw this, myself.

But the deliberate shooting of wounded men

and stretcher-bearers has been, so far as I know, confined to the Hun. On numerous occasions, some of which are mentioned elsewhere in this story, German snipers deliberately and in cold blood shot down our helpless wounded and the men who were endeavoring to succor them.

CHAPTER V

At Captain's Post

THE Battle of Loos had opened on the twenty-fifth of September and, although it was a considerable distance to the south of us, we had been hearing the continuous rumble of the guns ever since we had come up to the line. It was the first time we had heard "drum-fire," as the French call it. It is such an incessant bombardment, with such a large number of guns, that you can not distinguish any single reports, but the whole makes a continual "rumble," something like the roll of heavy thunder in the distance; never slacking, night or day. I have forgotten just how many days they kept it up, but it was something like two weeks.

To create a diversion, and prevent the enemy from taking troops from other parts of the line to strengthen the attacked point, our artillery, all along the line, was doing its best and our infantry made feint attacks at several places. We had gone back in the line on the first of October and, early the next morning, our brigade, Fourth Canadian, took part in one of these attacks. Our battalion did not go "over the top," but Bouchard and I stuck our gun up on the parapet and helped support the advance, which was made by the Nineteenth Battalion. It was our first experience of that kind and was, to say the least, interesting. The enemy kept up an incessant rifle and machine-gun fire on our position, the bullets were snapping around our heads like a bunch of fire-crackers and the mud was flying everywhere, but that little seventeen-year-old "kid" kept feeding in belts and all the while whooping and laughing like a maniac. It certainly cheered me up to have him there. The whole thing was over in about twenty minutes but, during that short time, we had learned something which can be learned in no other way—that it is possible for thousands of bullets to come close to you without doing any harm. From that time on, neither Bouchard nor I ever felt the least hesitation about slipping over the parapet at night to "see what we could see."

During this tour we were subjected to considerably more shelling than on the first occasion, and one morning Fritz made a mistake with one of his shells intended for "our farm," as we called the buildings in the rear, and dropped it "ker-plunk" right into one of our dug-outs. It was a place we had fixed up for cooking, and we were all outside, but it certainly made a mess of our "kitchen furniture." Then they shot up our communication trench until it was positively dangerous to go up and down it for rations and ammunition. Narrow escapes were numerous, but our luck held, and we went out the night of the eighth without having sustained a casualty. The battalion did not fare so well, having quite a number of wounded, but none killed.

That was our last visit to those trenches, as we marched, that night, away to the northward. "Eéps" was the word that went up and down the line, that being the Flemish pronunciation of Ypres, (in French pronounced "Eé-pr" and

AT CAPTAIN'S POST

in Tommy's English, "Wipers"). We had a hard
march; in the rain, as usual; and, about daylight,
stopped at the town of LaClytte, which was to
be the battalion's billeting place for several
months. The rest of the battalion remained there
a few days, resting, but the Emma Gees
went on ahead and took over some support
positions at Groot Vierstraat and along the Ypres-
Neuve Eglise road. We relieved the King Ed-
ward Horse who were acting, as was all the
cavalry, as infantry.

My crew, together with Sandy McNab's, was
assigned to an old Belgian farm called Captain's
Post. The place was pretty well shot up but
we managed to clear out enough room to give us
very good quarters; by far the best we had had
since leaving England. We were some 1,250
yards from the enemy lines but in plain sight
of them, hence it was necessary to be very careful not to allow any one to move about outside
the buildings in daytime, nor to make any smoke.

No doubt some one got careless, for about noon
the next day we heard the long-drawn-out

63

"who-o-o-o-i-s-s-s-h" of a big shell coming. It
struck about twenty-five yards behind our building and failed to explode; in soldier's parlance,
it was a "dud." We were eating dinner and
refused to be disturbed. Then came a steady
stream of the big fellows; to the right, to the left,
in front of the building and, finally, "smack,"
right into the house. Altogether, they put thirty-
two "five-point-nine" (150 mm.) shells into that
one old building and all the damage they did was
to ruin our dinner by filling the "dixie" with mud.
How in the world we escaped has always
been a mystery to me, but later on, after
other and worse affairs, the men called it
"McBride's luck." They shelled us pretty
regularly, after that, sometimes just two or
three shells, but on at least one occasion, they
evidently had made up their minds to put the
place out of business entirely, for they kept up
a continuous bombardment, with guns of at least
three calibers, for more than an hour. At that
time I was a corporal and had twelve men, with
two guns at this place, yet, although nearly every

Canadians with Machine Gun Taking Up New Positions

one was hit by pieces of brick and mud and covered with dust, not a man was hurt nor a gun injured.

One morning, just after daylight and during a fog, I was up in an old hay-loft where we had a gun, when I heard a cock pheasant "squawking" (that's the only word that describes it), out in front. Looking from the gun position I saw him, standing on the parapet of an abandoned French trench across the road. I could not resist the temptation, so took a shot at him, with the result that we had pheasant stew for dinner that day.

It was a source of never-ceasing wonder to me that the birds and other forms of wild life seemed to be so little affected by the continual noise of guns and shells. So far as I could notice they did not pay the slightest attention to it. Pheasants, partridges and rabbits were numerous at one point in and behind our lines and I have seen them running about, feeding or playing where shells were falling and bursting all about them, without showing any sign of fear. Indeed

they were sometimes killed by the shells, especially
shrapnel, but those unhit would "carry on" with
the business in hand, indifferent to the fate of
their companions.

The little robin redbreasts (the English
robin and the French *rouge-gorge*) were
abundant, as were the ubiquitous English sparrows, which, sitting out in front on the barbed
wire, were often used as targets by men firing
experimental shots.

A pair of swallows reared a family of young in
a dug-out which I once occupied, the nest being
within a few feet of my head when I was in
my bunk. They would come in and go out
through a small hole which we left in the burlap
curtain and the old bird would sit on the nest
and look at me in such a confidential, unafraid
sort of way that she made a friend for life and
I would have fought any one who had attempted to disturb or injure her. But, of course,
no such thing was possible. All the men seemed
to take a kindly interest in the birds and, except
for the occasional shot at the English sparrows

AT CAPTAIN'S POST

(which never hit them, anyhow), they rarely, if
ever, molested any of them unless it was for the
purpose of getting a meal of pheasant or part-
ridge, which was considered perfectly legitimate
although forbidden by "orders." It was all right
if you could "get away with it," as the saying is.

One morning, after an unusually intense bombardment of a wood called the Bois Carré, I
found many dead birds; killed either by direct
hits or by the concussion of the heavy shells.
This same morning I watched a pair of magpies
who were building a nest in a tree near our station. A shell had struck the tree, below the nest,
and had cut it in half while a large branch had
lodged just above the nest. The whole thing was
swaying dangerously in the light breeze and a
strong wind would surely bring it down, but that
pair of chattering magpies appeared to be debat-
ing whether to continue their work or move elsewhere. One would hop down to the place where
the shell had hit and, cocking his head
this way and that, would let loose a flow
of magpie talk that would bring his mate to him

and then they would both investigate, flying to the shattered place, clinging to the bark and picking out splinters and pieces of wood. Then they would go up aloft and consult about the nest itself. I watched them for the better part of an hour when the verdict appeared to be to "take a chance" and go ahead with the building. We left that place soon after and I never learned the final outcome.

At one point, where our lines were about one hundred yards from the enemy, there was a small pond in No Man's Land just outside our wire, and a pair of ducks, teal, I think, made it their home during the entire winter of 1915-16. In spite of the fact that shells were continually falling all around and sometimes bursting squarely in the pond itself, they never showed the least inclination to abandon the place. As this pond was surrounded by a fringe of small willows we often made use of the cover they afforded to make night reconnoissances, but soon learned that it was impossible to approach the pool without alarming the ducks and drawing from them a low scolding note of protest, accompanied by a splashing of water. This was carefully noted and, thereafter, all sentries at that point were especially warned to listen intently for these noises as it would probably mean that an enemy patrol was exploring in the vicinity.

The abandoning of so many of the farms and villages left a great many cats without homes. Nearly every ruined barn or house sheltered one or more of them and they were, as a rule, quite wild. Some, however, had been caught and tamed by the soldiers who made great pets of them. Frequently a soldier would be seen going in or out of the front line with a kitten perched contentedly on top of his pack. There was one big brindle "madame" cat who adopted our machine gun outfit when we first went in. She traveled up and down the line but never stayed anywhere except in one of the machine gun emplacements. On bright days she would hop up on top of the parapet and sit there, making her toilet, and then stretch out on the sand-bags for a nap. At this point it was not possible to show a hand or a periscope or any other small object without drawing the fire of some alert boche, but they never shot at the cat. I don't know why, superstition, perhaps.

This old cat had two litters of kittens while she was a "member" of our section and they were all grabbed up as soon as weaned, by both officers and men alike. It is simply human nature to want to have a pet of some kind and, as it was forbidden to take dogs into the lines, the soldiers turned to the cats. Of course they were of some use in killing mice, but the real scourge of the trenches, the giant rats, were too big and strong for any cat to tackle. There were literally millions of these rats. At night they appeared to be everywhere. They would eat up any rations that were left within reach and, boldly entering the dug-outs, would run about all over the sleeping men. It is decidedly unpleasant to be awakened to find one of these fellows perched on your chest and "sniff-sniff-sniffing" in your face. The men killed them in all sorts of ways, one of the most popular of which was to stick a bit of cheese on the end of the bayonet and, holding it down along the bottom of the trench, wait until Mr. Rat went after the cheese and then fire the rifle. Needless to say that rat was "na-poo," which is soldier-French, meaning "finis."

At Captain's Post a cat had a family of kittens, just learning to walk, hidden in a haymow, when we were shelled unmercifully. After the bombardment ceased, upon going up into the mow to inspect the damage, I found them. They were all covered with brick-dust but unhurt. By actual count, no less than five shells had burst within ten feet of the nest in which they were hidden; in fact, the whole place was an utter ruin, yet they came through it untouched. Then, at Sniper's Barn there was a big black cat, wild as a fox, which had a hiding-place somewhere among the ruins of the upper story. I had a sniping nest, burrowed under a lot of tobacco which had been stored there, and was occupying it one day when the Germans shelled the place. They put several shells into that part of the building, cutting the legs off the tripod of my telescope and burying the whole works, including myself. But what interested and amused me most was when a shell rooted out that cat and sent it flying down into my quarters, unhurt but so plastered with dust from the bricks and mortar that no one would have ever suspected it of being black. It was an entirely new variety—a red cat. It sat and looked at me for a long time. Disgust, just plain, every-day disgust, was written all over that animal's face. I don't know what would have happened had I not laughed. I simply could not help it, the sight was so funny. With my first shout the cat seemed to "come to" and, with a terrified yowl, sped through a narrow opening and took to the woods.

To change the subject: Many of our men will, doubtless, be comforted to know that in one respect Flanders is like Ireland—there are no snakes.

One of our guns on this line was in the upper story of an old brewery at Vierstraat, about seven hundred yards from my position, and we occasionally exchanged visits. One day, I was down there talking with the boys when a five-inch (sixty pounder) shrapnel shell burst in front of the building, the case coming right on through, into the room where we were. It "scooted," glanced, ricochetted, or whatever you want to call it, all around that room and you never saw such a scampering to get out. It finally stopped, however, and one of the boys dragged it out into the light for an examination. On the side it was branded "BEARDMORE, SCOTLAND." Now, how do you suppose Heinie got that?

CHAPTER VI

OUR OWN CHEERFUL FASHION

ON October twelfth there was a general attack along our front, to try out some new "smoke bombs" and shells. It was the first time the smoke barrage was used. We took our guns down about half-way to the front line and set them up in hedge-rows and other places where we could sweep the front in case the enemy made a counter-attack and got into our lines. However, we were not needed, so remained spectators of about as pretty a show as I have ever seen. At a given signal, every gun behind our lines dropped smoke shells in a continuous row along the line, just in front of the enemy's parapet. As each shell struck, it burst, sending out great streamers of white smoke that soon became a dense wall through which no one could see. Under cover of this, our bombers advanced, threw hand grenades into the enemy trenches and then retired. No attempt was made to take any part of the line; it was more in the nature of a try-out for the new shells and also for the purpose of harassing the enemy.

Naturally, the boche, expecting a general attack, commenced to shell everything in that part of the country and also opened up a heavy machine-gun and rifle fire, a good deal of which came our way, but no one was hit. On the way back to the barn, Bouchard and I were walking side by side, perhaps three or four feet apart, when a "whizz-bang" came right between us and struck the ground not more than ten feet in front. In nine hundred and ninety-nine cases out of a thousand that would have spelled our finish, but the shell struck on the edge of a little hump, at the side of a ditch, turned sidewise and spun round like a top. We stood there, speechless, fascinated by the peculiar antics of the thing, until it stopped. It was a pretty toy, a 105 mm., painted red and with a beautiful brass fuse-cap. I picked it up but as it was too hot to handle I put on my asbestos gloves, used for changing barrels of machine guns, and carried it "home" where I put it away, intending to get some artilleryman to remove the fuse and explosive so that I might keep it as a souvenir; but a bunch of boys from the Eighteenth Battalion found it, and taking it back to their dug-out at Ridgewood, tried to unload it themselves. Some were killed and several wounded when the thing exploded. I afterward saw one of those who had been wounded and he told me about it.

At this stage of the soldier's career he is always a "souvenir hunter," picking up and carrying around with him all sorts of things, from German bullets to big shells. I was a fiend of the first magnitude and collected enough stuff to stock a museum, only to have to abandon it whenever we moved. I had French rifles, bayonets and other equipment; German ditto and about every size and type of shell and fuse that was used on our front. Whenever we moved I would bury or cache the whole lot, in the hope that I could get back for it some day. But the fever finally wore off, and I got so that

OUR OWN CHEERFUL FASHION

I would not even pick up a German helmet. Now, of course, I wish I had some of that stuff to show the folks.

On the fifteenth of October we went into the front line; a line which we, alternating with the Twentieth Battalion, were destined to hold until the following April. About this time the rains set in "for keeps" and we were seldom dry or warm or clean for nearly six months. Mud, mud, nothing but mud—mud without any bottom. We had no trenches, proper; they were simply sand-bag barricades between us and the enemy and it was a continual struggle to keep them built up. They would ooze away like melting butter.

When the deadlock came, in the fall of 1914, and the opposing armies lay entrenched, from the North Sea to Switzerland, it found the Germans occupying the dominating heights, with our forces hanging on, as best they could, to positions on the lower ground.

This was the case at the point where we were located. Our sector (about eleven hundred yards

77

for the battalion frontage) extended from the Voormezeele-Wytschaete road, northward to the bottom of the hill at the top of which was the village of St. Eloi. Directly opposite our left was Piccadilly Farm, located on a hill about ten meters higher than our lines. From there toward the right, the enemy line gradually descended until, at the right of our line, it was only about two meters higher. The distance between the front lines varied from about seventy yards, at the right, to about two hundred and fifty yards at the left. The net result of this situation was that the Germans could dig trenches of considerable depth, draining the water out under their parapets or into two small streams which ran from their lines to ours. They had a playful habit of damming up these streams until an unusually hard rain would come, when they would open the gates and give us the benefit of the whole dose. I have seen the water in these streams rise seven feet within less than an hour and there were times when in one of our communication trenches it was over a man's head. A soldier of the West

OUR OWN CHEERFUL FASHION

York's regiment was drowned in this trench one night.

Under such conditions, it was impossible for us to dig. All we could do was to construct sand-bag parapets or barricades, while our so-called "dug-outs" consisted of huts constructed of sand-bags, roofed with corrugated iron and covered with more sand-bags. They afforded protection from shrapnel and small shell fragments, but, of course, not against direct hits from any kind of shells. Even a little "whizz-bang" would go through them as though they were egg-shells. All the earth thereabouts was of the consistency of thick soup and our parapet had a habit of sloughing away just about as fast as we could build it up. As a matter of fact, our communication trenches did become completely obliterated and we had no recourse but to go in and out of the trenches "overland." At night this was not so bad, although we were continually losing men from stray bullets. But when it was necessary, as it sometimes was, to go in or out in daylight why, it was a

cinch that some one was going to get hit, as the
enemy had many good snipers watching for just
such opportunities. At one time, for over two
weeks more than two hundred yards of our
parapet were down, and if you went from one
end of the line to the other you must expose your-
self to the full view of enemy snipers. My duties
required me to cover this stretch of trench at
least twice a day.

Our conduct in taking short cuts across the
fields when the trenches were knee-deep with mud,
was scandalous in the eyes of our neighbors of
the Imperial army, as the troops from the British
Isles are known. Quite frequently we were
subjected to the most scathing tongue-lashing
from officers of the old school, but we won the
astonished admiration of the Tommies by our dis-
regard of instructions and advice. I well remember one day when a party of us were
going out through the P. & O. communication
trench and, finding the mud too deep, we climbed
out and walked across the open, whereat an old
Colonel of some Highland regiment gave us a

OUR OWN CHEERFUL FASHION

"beautiful calling." His discourse was a master-piece of fluent soldier talk and, as a Scot usually does when excited, he lapsed into the "twa-talk" of his native Hielans. I can remember his last words, which were to the effect that: "Ye daft Cany-deens think ye're awfu' brave but I tell ye the noo it's no bravery; it's sheer stupidity." Of course he was right, but we could not allow the small matter of a bullet or two to stand in the way of our getting out in time for tea, and finally they gave it up in disgust and allowed us to "go to hell in our own cheerful fashion," as they said.

With the assistance of the engineers, we finally succeeded in constructing a new line, slightly in the rear of the old one which was abandoned except for a couple of machine-gun positions and a listening post. We also managed to get out a fairly good barbed-wire entanglement along most of the front. Fritz appeared to be having his troubles, too, so did not bother us much at night. We always got a few shells every day and usually quite a number of rifle grenades and "fish-tail" aerial torpedoes, but they did very little damage.   Here was where the mud was our friend, for, unless a shell dropped squarely on the top of you, it would do no harm.

CHAPTER VII

SNIPER'S BARN

JUST as streets and roads must have their names, so must all trenches have official designations. This applies also to localities, farms, cross-roads, woods and such places which have no "regular" names or which possess Flemish or French names difficult of pronunciation by the soldiers.

Front-line trenches are usually designated by letters or numbers, running in regular order, from right to left in each sector. Certain important points may have special names. Communication trenches are always given distinctive names. Probably the majority of these names are those of prominent streets and roads in England, especially in London. At Messines we had "Surrey Lane," "Stanley Road" and "Plum Avenue" for communication trenches, while our front line embraced the whole series of "C" trenches. During

83

the winter we occupied the "N" and "O" front-
line trenches, while our communication trenches
bore such names as "Poppy Lane," "Bois Carré"
(afterward called "Chicory Trench" because it
ran through a chicory field), and the "P. & O."
so named because it entered the front line at the
junction of the "O" and "P" trenches and P. &
O. is so much easier to say than O. & P.   At
St. Eloi, "Convent Lane" and "Queen Victoria
Street" were examples of the communication
trenches, while the front-line positions were designated by numbers, as elsewhere explained.   Originally, they were called the "Q" and "R" trenches.
Opposite Hill 60 (so named because it is sixty
meters above sea level), the numbering method
was continued in the front line, while the communication trenches included "Petticoat Lane,"
"Fleet Street" and "Rat Alley."   At various places
along the lines you would find "Marble Arch,"
"Highgate," "Piccadilly Circus," and so on.

Supporting points were generally designated
as "S. P. 7" (or other number), or as "Redoubts" with identifying names.   In one place we

WYTSCHAETE MAP

The reproduction on the opposite page is a section from the map known as Wytschaete. Here are Shelley Farm, White Horse Cellars and St. Eloi, with the British front line shown by faint dashes, crossing the road that runs through White Horse Cellars, at figure 2. The German trenches, indicated by irregular black lines, are close to the British front at this point, but run sharply away down to Piccadilly Farm and beyond on the left. The trenches on this map are corrected to February 20th, 1916. Sniper's Barn that figures so thrillingly in Captain McBride's experiences is shown at the extreme left of the map, only the word Barn appearing.

SNIPER'S BARN

had the "Southern, Eastern and Western" redoubts along the edges of a certain wood.

Sometimes the original Flemish names were
retained for the farms, châteaux and cross-roads,
but more often they would be Anglicized by
our map makers. Thus we had "Moated Grange,"
"Bus House," "Shelley Farm," "Beggar's
Rest," "Dead Dog Farm," "Sniper's Barn,"
"Captain's Post," "Maple Copse," the "White
Château" and the "Red Château," "Dead Horse
Corner," "White Horse Cellars" and so on, in-
definitely. "Scottish Wood" was so named for
the London Scottish who made a famous charge
there in the early part of the war. Hallebast
Corner was changed by the soldier to "Hell-
blast" Corner, just as Ypres became "Wipers" and
Ploegstert was translated into "Plugstreet." As
to the estaminets, (drinking places), while
many retained their original names, such as
"Pomme d'Or," "Repos aux Voyageurs" or
"Herberg in der Kruisstraat," such names as
"The Pig & Whistle" and "Cheshire Cheese"
were not uncommon.

THE EMMA GEES

"Shrapnel Corners" and "Suicide Corners" were numerous and had merely a local significance. The names are self-explanatory. "Gordon Farm," where the Gordon Highlanders had stopped for a time, and "School Farm," where we had a bombing and machine-gun school, were other examples. "Hyde Park Corner," afterward changed to "Canada Corner," was an important junction point of the roads back of our lines. "Bedford House" was a name given to a château which the Bedfords once occupied. It would require a large book to enumerate them all.

Our line was at the exact spot where the Princess Pat's first went into action and several of them were buried in our trenches, together with many others, both French and English. In fact, it was difficult to dig anywhere for earth to fill sand-bags without uncovering bodies. The whole place was nothing more nor less than one continuous grave. There were a great many crosses, put up by comrades, giving name, date and organization, but hundreds had no mark other

than the cross, sometimes inscribed "an unknown
soldier," but more often unmarked. Here one
of our sergeants found the grave of his brother,
who had been serving in the King's Royal Rifles
and I noticed another cross near by marked with
the name of Meyers, Indianapolis, Indiana,
said to have been the first man of the Princess
Pat's killed in action. There was a maze
of old French and English trenches, some
in front of our line and some behind it and all
more or less filled with bodies that had
never been buried. Some of the Indian troops
had fought here and had left many of their number behind. Whenever it was possible, we buried
the bodies, but often they were in such positions
that this was impossible and any attempt to do
so would only have resulted in further losses. I
nearly forgot to mention it; but there were plenty
of Germans mixed up with the lot; in one small
area, just in front of a farm building, some five
hundred yards in our rear, I found eight of them.
Inside the building was a dead French soldier who,
as we figured it out, had accounted for the eight

boches before they got him. This place was called Sniper's Barn.

While our artillery had been considerably increased, it was still far below that of the enemy in number or size of guns, and the ammunition supply was so short that each gun was limited to a very few rounds a day. It was only during the following summer that the English caught up with the Germans in artillery. This, naturally, did not tend to cheer up the men. It was aggravating, to say the least, to have the other fellow sending over "crumps" without limit, and be able to send back nothing but six or eight "whizz-bangs." ("Crump" is the general name for high-explosive shells of from 4.1 up, but the commonest size is the 5.9 or 150 mm.)

Having been so successful at the strafing at Messines, our Colonel was anxious that we continue the game here and I was delegated to locate a good position and "go to it." After going over all the ground back of our lines, I decided to try the experiment of placing the gun in a small hedge which ran across the lower end of an old garden or orchard, in front of Sniper's Barn;

that is, on the side toward the enemy. It looked rather foolhardy, at first glance, for the place was in plain sight from the German lines and only about five hundred yards away at the nearest point; but I remembered our experience at our first strafing place and depended on Heinie to jump to the conclusion that we were in the farm buildings, and devote his attention to them. It worked; he "ran true to form," as a race horse man would say, and while we maintained a gun, and sometimes two, in that place for six months, and the boche shot up the barn regularly during all that time, there was never a shell, apparently, directed at our position, and except for an occasional "short," none burst near us.

From there we would shoot, day and night, often, at the first, having our targets where we could "see 'em fall," a very unusual occurrence for a machine gunner, save during a general engagement. Of course we would have to get into the position before daylight and remain until dark as the way to and from it was exposed to view from "across the way."

Here we worked out many of the constantly

89

recurring problems which confront the machine gunner in the field, and which are, as a rule, overlooked or neglected during the preliminary training. As our own soldiers will have to contend with the same conditions, I may mention some of them.

One of the first things we discovered was that while all the small-arms ammunition issued was made pursuant to uniform specifications, furnished by the War Office, a large percentage of it was manufactured in new, hastily equipped factories, by partially trained workmen, and while it was apparently near enough to the standard to pass the tests exacted by the inspectors, only an extremely small proportion would function properly in machine guns or other automatic arms. A few of the old standard brands, made in government arsenals or by the prominent, long-established private manufacturers, could be depended upon at all times, but, unfortunately, these brands were comparatively scarce and hard to get. At least seventy-five per cent. of what we received was the product of the small, new and ill-equipped factories, established under the press of war demands, and, while it appeared to work satisfactorily in the ordinary rifles, both Enfield and Ross, it was utterly useless for machine guns. The difference of a minute fraction of an inch in the thickness of the "rim" would break extractors as fast as they could be replaced, while various other irregularities, so small as to be undiscoverable without the most accurate measurements by delicate micrometers, would cause stoppages and the breaking of different small parts. And, at that time, spare parts were almost unknown, so it required the utmost ingenuity on the part of the gunners to improvise, with what materials could be found on the spot, and with the very few tools at hand, many of the small but all-important parts that go to make up the interior economy of the guns.

All automatically operated firearms are, of necessity, very delicately balanced mechanisms. Whether gas or recoil operated, there must be just sufficient power obtained from the firing of one shot to overcome the normal friction of the

working parts, eject the empty cartridge case
withdraw a new cartridge from the belt or magazine, load it properly in the chamber and fire it
continuing this action as long as the trigger, or
other firing device, is kept pressed or until the
belt or magazine is emptied. Ammunition which
does not give the proper amount of pressure or
cartridges which, through faulty manufacture,
cause an undue amount of friction, either in seating them in the chamber, withdrawing them from
the belt or in removing the fired case, will not
operate the gun properly and will cause "jams."
On the other hand, ammunition which develops
too much pressure or creates too little friction,
will cause breakages because of the excess jar and
hammering of the moving parts.

We utilized parts of cream separators, sewing
machines, baby carriages, bicycles and various
agricultural implements, found in and around the
old Belgian farms, and it soon became common
talk that we could make every part of a machine
gun excepting the barrel. We learned that there
was a certain bolt, a part of the rifle carrier on the

SNIPER'S BARN

French bicycle, which was an exact duplicate of an important part of our guns, so, whenever we found one of those old, broken and abandoned cycles, we would take time to remove this particular part and carry it along for emergencies. This is but one instance of many.

Then, there was the matter of concealing the flash, when firing at night. As the position we occupied was in plain view of the enemy lines, to have fired without some device to prevent the flash being seen would, inevitably, have resulted in a concentration of fire upon us which would have rendered the position untenable. We tried many schemes, from the crude "sand-bag" screen to the most elaborate devices made in the armorer's shops, while back in billets, and finally perfected one which was thoroughly satisfactory. I can not describe it here, as I hope to see it used by our soldiers in France, but I can say that, out of probably fifty different contrivances made for the same purpose, this was the only one that "filled the bill" from every standpoint.

As most of our firing was done at night, it was

necessary to improve the manner of mounting and "laying" the guns as we soon found that the methods taught at the training schools and the lamps and other mechanical devices furnished by the authorities were of no use under actual service conditions.

The various schemes and devices which we originated and elaborated are at the disposal of the proper military authorities in this country but, obviously, can not be described here.

The foreign officers, British and French, who are now in this country acting as instructors and advisers are doing everything in their power to impress upon our officers and men the necessity for keeping up to date in all the various and complicated departments of military training, even to the exclusion of many of the pet ideas of some of the most accomplished instructors in our service schools. The trouble with us is that we have not, and never have had, any machine gunners in the United States Army. By this I mean men skilled in machine gunnery as applied to present-day warfare. The evolution of machine-gun tactics is,

SNIPER'S BARN

perhaps, the most outstanding feature of the whole war. From being, as it was considered four years ago, merely an emergency weapon or, as the text-book writers were pleased to call it, "a weapon of opportunity," it has become the most important single weapon in use in any army, not even excepting the artillery. A properly directed machine-gun barrage is far more difficult to traverse than anything the artillery can put down and the combination of artillery and machine guns, working together, whether on the offensive or defensive, represents the highest point ever attained in the effective use of fire in battle.

Our instructors have been technical theorists of the very highest order, basing their theories and working out their problems on the experience furnished by previous wars and of course it is difficult for them to realize that nearly every hypothesis which they have assumed in working out their theories has been proved false. They can not believe that "fire control" of infantry, as taught in the school of fire, has no place in modern trench warfare. It will break the hearts of some of them to learn that the ability to read a map and use a prismatic compass is of far more value than knowledge of the "mil-scale" or "fire-control rule." They will probably be scandalized by the statement, which I make seriously and with full knowledge whereof I speak, that one common shovel and an armful of sand-bags are worth more than all the range-finders that have been or ever will be bought for the use of machine gunners.

Every foot of ground in France, Belgium and Germany has been so thoroughly and accurately mapped that there need be no such thing as estimating ranges. You *know* the range; you do not have to depend on mental or mechanical estimates. And, as machine-gun fire is almost entirely indirect fire, the guns must be laid by using map, compass, protractor and clinometer (quadrant), in exactly the same manner as ar-tillery fire is directed. The average machine gunner will probably go through the whole war without ever seeing a live enemy—excepting prisoners. The various methods of controlling

Highlanders with a Maxim Gun

indirect fire by resection, base lines and observation from two or more points are, like the use of an auxiliary aiming point, useless in trench warfare. They are fine in theory and afford much interesting diversion on the training ranges, but when you go to war, why, it can't be done, that's all.

This is a common, plain, hard-headed business proposition: where the only idea is to kill as many of the enemy as possible before he kills you, it has been found that the oldest, crudest and most primitive methods have, in many cases, proved the most effective for the attainment of this end.

Never before has it been of such vital importance to train the individual soldier, whether he be rifleman, bomber, machine gunner or any other specialist, so that he can "carry on" without the direction of an officer. The officer must plan everything in advance; he must look after the health and comfort of his men, see that they are properly equipped and supplied, must station them in their appointed positions, make frequent

97

personal inspections and, finally, lead them in the advance. But in every engagement there comes a time when every man is "on his own," when it is impossible for the officer, if he be still living, to direct the action. The idea that an officer can exercise "fire control" as taught in our service schools, or can personally direct the fire of a number of machine guns, once the action has started, is ridiculous. The limits of one man's sphere of action, at such a time, are extremely small. If the men have been properly instructed, beforehand, and then given a good start, they will do the rest. It is just this ability to assimilate individual instruction that has made the Canadian superior to the native-born Briton. He is better educated, as a rule, has lived a freer and more varied life and, as a result, possesses that initiative and individual ingenuity which are so often necessary at the critical stages of a fight. We have every reason to expect that the American soldier, for these same reasons, will prove to be at least the equal of the Canadian—the finest type of fighting man yet developed by this war.

CHAPTER VIII

Getting the Flag

WE soon fell into the routine of moving; from front line to support; from support to the front line and back to reserve. For some time these movements were uncertain but we finally settled down to a regular schedule, which was maintained, with few breaks, throughout the winter. When the time came to go into the reserve, the rest of the battalion would go back to LaClytte but the Emma Gees went only to the Vierstraat-Brasserie line before described. From there detachments would alternate in going back to the battalion billets for a bath and clean clothing. Some of us rigged up our own bath house in Captain's Post, so found it unnecessary to go any farther. Personally, there was only one day in three months when I was out of sight of the German lines. We had comfortable quarters where we were and the towns of Dickebusch and LaClytte had no attractions for me; and as to the battalion billets, they were abominable. They consisted of so-called huts which were simply floors with roofs over them: no walls at all; just a sloping, tent-like roof on top of a rough board floor. Outside, they were partly banked up and plentifully smeared with mud, camouflaged, as it were. The British made it a practise at that time to keep their troops out of the inhabited towns that were within range of the enemy's guns, so as not to give any excuse for shelling them. LaClytte was a very small town of but a few hundred native inhabitants, but Dickebusch, situated about midway between the lines and LaClytte, was a city of several thousands. In both places were hundreds of refugees from the ruined towns to the eastward.

However, it seemed to make little difference to the boche; he shelled both towns, intermittently, killing a number of civilians but very rarely hitting a soldier. Later, in the spring of 1916, they started in to wipe out Dickebusch, and, for all practical purposes, they succeeded. I will speak of this in a later chapter.

GETTING THE FLAG

Where opposing lines are so close together, say less than one hundred yards apart, and the ground is level and star shells are going up almost continuously, it would seem to be nearly an impossibility for any man or number of men to venture out into No Man's Land without being seen and fired upon by the enemy. But with certain members of each organization it is merely a part of the daily routine. Every night they slip over the parapet and, in small groups, patrol up and down the line, constantly on the alert to prevent any surprise attack by the enemy. But this is not all. There are times, at all points, when it is necessary to put out new barbed wire or repair the old; when large parties of men must go out there and work for hours, within a stone's throw of a vigilant and merciless enemy. Occasionally they are discovered and have trouble, but in the great majority of cases the work is done and every one gets back unhurt.

How is it done? Simply a matter of training and careful preparation. Every man is rehearsed in his work until he can do it perfectly, quickly and without noise. Materials are carefully checked up and distributed and, each man having a certain specified task and no other, there is no confusion or blundering. They all know that, when a flare goes up near by, they must "freeze" in whatever position they may be. Movements of any kind would be sure to discover them to the enemy lookout, but lacking that movement it is a hundred-to-one shot they will be undetected.

There have been a good many instances where a flag has been planted by the enemy, on his parapets or inside his wire, with a challenge to any one to come over and get it. There was one such opposite our position. Many stories had been told about that flag: The Brandenburgers had it first, then the French got it and passed it along to the English, who relieved them; then the Prussians took it away from the British and had held it ever since; for about a year, in fact. We could see it, plainly enough; a dark blue affair with some sort of a device in yellow in the center. I often noticed it from our position back at Sniper's Barn and had some rather hazy ideas about going over after it.

One dark rainy night in November, a man in the section named Lucky announced that he was going over to Fritz's line to try to locate a new machine-gun emplacement which we had reason to believe had been recently constructed. He slipped over the parapet where a road ran through our lines and those of the enemy. It was only about seventy yards across at this point.

Working his way through our wire, he crawled along the side of the old disused road, there being a shallow ditch there which afforded a little concealment. The flares were going up frequently and progress was, of course, very slow. At one place the body of a soldier was lying in the ditch and, in trying to roll it out of the way, he pulled off one of the feet. By creeping along, inch by inch, he finally reached the enemy's wire and spent about an hour working through it. Then crawling along the outside of the parapet, stopping often to listen, he soon found the loophole of the new gun emplacement. Taking a sheet of paper which he had brought for the purpose, he fastened it directly below the loophole where it would be in plain sight from our lines but invisible to the occupants of the place. His work done, he was about to start back when he happened to think of that flag and concluded to have a try for it. It was probably a hundred yards or more down the trench from where he then was and it required the utmost care to avoid making a noise as the front of the parapet, as is always the case, was thickly strewn with tin cans and rubbish of all sorts. Lucky had been a big game hunter in Canada, however, and had even stalked the wily moose which is about the last word in "still hunting," so he managed to negotiate the distance without detection and finally reached the flag.

Carefully feeling up along the staff, he discovered that it was anchored with wires which ran into the ground and then he remembered the tales that had been told of how it was attached to a bomb or small mine which would be exploded if the flagstaff were disturbed. That was a

GETTING THE FLAG

common German trick and not at all unlikely in
this case, but, after thinking the matter over, he
decided to make an attempt to unfasten the wires.
This did not take long, after which all that remained was to pull out the staff and "beat it."
Taking his pistol in his right hand, to be ready for
emergencies, and reaching up with the left, he gave
the pole a sharp jerk. Well, there must have been
another wire, somewhere, connected up with two
"fixed rifles," aimed directly at the stick for,
when he pulled on it, two rifle reports rang out
and two bullets hit the flagstaff, cutting it off
just below his hand which was also slightly cut.
Quickly rolling down into a slight depression he
hugged the flag to him and lay quiet, while the
Germans, aroused by the shots, immediately
opened fire with rifles, which were soon joined by
a machine gun. They could not hit him where he
was so he just lay still and waited. Suddenly,
without warning, they fired a flare light directly
over his head. He told me afterward that was the
only time he was really scared. He thought it was
a bomb. However that soon passed and, the firing

having died down, he made his way back to our lines with the flag which he gave to the Colonel the next morning. "And they gave him a medal for that."

On another occasion, one of our scouts made his way through the German line and having located a battery in the rear, started back, only to discover that the place where he had come over was now occupied by several soldiers, and, being unable to find another opening, was obliged to hide out and remain inside the enemy's lines all day. The next night he managed to slip back, none the worse for his adventure.

Such things are being done every night and some men consider it the greatest sport in the world to go out alone and spend hours under the lee of a German parapet listening to the Heinies talk. Soon after that, orders were issued in our brigade that no one was to go out alone so when we wanted to prowl around we had to start in pairs. As soon as we were over the parapet we would split and each go his way, to meet later at an appointed place. One man, alone, can get

away with a lot of things that would be impossible for two, but we observed the letter, if not
the spirit, of the order.

We had cleared out one of the compartments of
the big barn at Captain's Post, carefully plugging
up all the shell-holes with sand-bags and other
materials so that no light could filter through, and
there, at night, would build a great fire in the
middle of the stone floor and proceed to enjoy ourselves. Usually one or two guns would do a little
strafing every night: simply going out into
the field in front of the building and setting up
the gun in a convenient shell-hole. After a while,
from our own observations and from information
supplied by the artillery, we occasionally located
an enemy battery within range of our guns.
Then we would have a regular "strafing party."
Laying all the guns so as to deliver a converging
fire on the battery position, we would, as soon as
it was dark, open up on them, knowing that
they would be moving about in the open and
exposed to fire. We could always tell when we
had "stung" them, for they would invariably

come back at us with a tremendous fire, shooting wildly at everything within our lines in the vain endeavor to locate us. I'll bet we caused them to expend a hundred thousand rounds of perfectly good ammunition in this way, but we never had a man hit while at the game. The German is not much of a hand for night artillery work unless you stir him up, but we could always get a rise out of him, and often did it, just for amusement. This is what is called "getting his wind up." The same thing can be done in the front line by a few men opening up with five or ten rounds, rapid fire, directed just over Heinie's parapet. In nearly every case, he will commence shooting blindly toward our lines: the contagion will spread and, the first thing you know, he will have wasted about a million rounds.

Here, as in most parts of the line, except during an engagement, cooking was done right in the front trenches. The method is to use a brazier made from an old iron bucket, punched full of holes, in which charcoal or coke is burned. As we seldom had charcoal, it was necessary to

A Light Vickers Gun in Action

start the fire before daylight, using wood to ignite
the coke which made no smoke but, with careful nursing, could be made to burn all day. The
presence of smoke always drew the fire of rifle
grenades, trench-mortar shells and even artillery.
It was one of our favorite forms of amusement to locate a cook house and shoot it
up; and when a shell made a direct hit, if, among
the pots and pans flying through the air, we
could distinguish a German cap or something that
looked like a part of a boche, there was much
rejoicing in our lines. Of course it was a game
at which two could play and we were not immune
by any means.

These little things helped to keep up the interest and break the monotony of the work. About
this time the famous Lahore Battery, from the
Indian city of that name, was added to the artillery behind our sector; and they appeared not to
be restricted in the number of rounds per day
which they were permitted to fire. I remember
the first time they did any shooting over our
heads. It was the day after they had "registered

in" that a large working party was discovered on Piccadilly Farm, directly opposite our left. When the F. O. O. (forward observing officer) was informed of it, he had a good look through his periscope binoculars and then called up the Lahore Battery and, without any preliminary ranging shots, ordered "forty rounds per gun." As they had six guns, they poured in the shells at the rate of about one hundred a minute and they certainly did make things fly in and about that farm.

CHAPTER IX

HUNTING HUNS

URING October the casualties in the Machine Gun Section were only three wounded, McNab, Redpath and Jack Lee all getting hit on the same day. They were sent back to England. At that time it was not considered the proper thing for a man to go back if he could, by any means, "carry on" and these three were all bitterly disappointed when they found that they would have to leave the section. There came a time, all too soon, when a "Blighty" was the finest present a man could get; the loss of a few fingers or even a hand or foot being considered not too high a price to pay to get out of hell for a few months.

When the weather was very bad there was but little sniping going on, so we often went in and out of the lines "overland" in broad daylight. Sunday, November fourteenth, was one such occasion. We had not been relieved until noon by the Twentieth Battalion who had taken a very roundabout way to get in, so I put it up to all my crowd to choose whether we should spend several hours going around or take a chance down the open road. They unanimously decided on the road, so I started out ahead, with instructions for them to follow at about fifty-yard intervals, and in this fashion we walked down at least four hundred yards of open road, every foot of which was in plain sight of the German lines, and got under cover of a small hill without a single shot being fired. From this point it was necessary to cross another small open space but, as it was partly screened by bushes and trees, we did not consider it dangerous.

We had a redoubt concealed in the small hill mentioned and I stopped to arrange about the relief of the gun crew stationed there. The remainder of the party, except Charlie Wendt, continued on their way and soon disappeared in the woods. Charlie stayed a few minutes and then said: "I'll go on ahead, Mac, and wait for you at the Eastern Redoubt." He started out

HUNTING HUNS

across the field and I continued my talk with
Endersby, who was in charge of the local gun,
when, all at once, I heard some one call out: "Oh,
Mac," and looked to see Wendt on the ground
about one hundred yards away waving his hand
to me. Endersby immediately ran to him and I
followed as soon as I could drop part of the
heavy load I was carrying. On reaching him I
found that he had been shot through the abdomen.
Just then another bullet snapped beside us, so I
told Endersby to get back to the redoubt and
telephone for stretcher-bearers, while I bandaged
the wound. Charlie remarked: "Well, they got
me, but I hope you get about ten of them for me."
I assured him that we would and told him to
keep his nerve and he would come through all
right. He was a very strong, clean-living young
man and I really thought he had a chance. He
did not think so, saying he was afraid the doctors
would have some difficulty in patching up such a
hole. He did not cry out nor make the slightest
complaint but kept assuring me that "everything
is all right."

THE EMMA GEES

Meantime, the sniper was keeping up a continuous fire, hitting everything in the neighborhood but me, at whom he was shooting. It was such a miserable exhibition of marksmanship—only about five hundred yards distant and a bright clear day—that I told Charlie I would be ashamed to have such a poor shot in our outfit. Any American soldier who could qualify as a marksman would scarcely miss such a target and a sharpshooter or expert rifleman would be forever disgraced if he made less than the highest possible score. However, I forgave that fellow; being a German he could not be expected to know how to shoot straight at any range beyond three hundred meters. The shot that hit Charlie was just a "luck shot," but that did not help much.

I tried to drag him along toward a slight depression, but it hurt him so I desisted and waited for the stretcher-bearers. When I saw them approaching I called a warning and had one of them crawl to us with the small trench stretcher, on which we managed to get Charlie into a sheltered place, where they shifted him to a long litter and started out with him. The last thing he said was: "It's all right, Mac; everything is all right; don't you worry."

They did all they could for him while I had to go back and get the machine gun that he had dropped. The fellow across the way showed perseverance, at any rate, and kept up his "schutzenfest" as long as I was in sight but without result.

Next day we learned that Charlie had died and was buried at Bailleul. He was not only one of the most popular men in the section, but was the first we had had killed and we all felt very much depressed. I got a permit to go to Bailleul to see whether or not he had been properly buried and there made my first acquaintance with the G. R. C. We had often seen those letters, followed by a number, on the crosses, in trenches, in cemeteries or along the roads, but none knew what they meant. At Bailleul I found the head office of the "Graves Registration Commission" and, within five minutes, knew where Wendt was buried and

the number of his grave. This wonderful organization undertakes to furnish a complete
record of the burial place of every soldier.
Where suitable crosses have not been provided, they furnish one, bearing an aluminum
plate showing the name, number, regiment and
date of death wherever this information is available. Now they have gone even further and are
compiling a photographic record of all known
graves so that relatives, writing to the Commission, can secure not only a verbal description but
an actual photograph of the loved one's grave.

I went back and began to plan ways and means
of "getting" Charlie's ten boches, but a day or two
later something happened to alter my scheme to a
certain extent.

At that time, our ration parties were going out
just before daylight, as we had no communication trench and had to cross the open and exposed
ground behind our line. The two, who went from
one of the guns, however, Dupuis and Lanning,
were a little bit late, so that it was light when they
started out. About fifty yards down the road

was a bend, afterward called the Devil's Elbow. From this point, they were in plain sight
from the enemy line and, no sooner had they
reached the Elbow than a sniper fired and got
Lanning through the lungs. As he fell, Dupuis
knelt down to assist, when he received a bullet
through the head, killing him instantly. One of
our detachment of stretcher-bearers (composed of
the members of our pipe band) was located but a
few yards away and, without hesitation, one of
the "Scotties" dashed out to help the fallen men.
He was instantly shot down, as were three others
in succession, who attempted to get to the spot.
By this time an officer arrived and prevented
more of the men from running out. This officer,
by crawling carefully down a shallow ditch alongside the road, managed with the assistance of a
sergeant to recover all the bodies. Four were
dead and two wounded, one of whom died a few
hours later. These stretcher-bearers were unarmed and wore the broad white brassard with the
red cross conspicuously displayed on their sleeves.
The sniper was only about one hundred yards

distant and could not possibly have failed to see this mark.

Then and there I registered a silent vow that these men, to paraphrase Kipling:

". . . should go to their God in state:
With fifty file of Germans, to open them Heaven's gate."

Later, I was to see other and worse happenings along that same road, but, at that time, I considered this as about the limit.

The officer who had done such splendid work in recovering the wounded men was himself killed about an hour later, together with one of his sergeants and two men, by a shrapnel shell. He was the first officer we had lost in the battalion, Lieutenant Wilgress, and had been very popular, with officers and men alike.

It was a sad day for us, that twenty-seventh of November, 1915, and yet it was one of those days when "there is nothing to report from the Ypres salient."

Next day I asked and received permission to go back a few miles to a sniper's school, where I

Canadian Machine Gun Section Getting Their Guns Into Action

got a specially targeted rifle, equipped with the finest kind of a telescopic sight. I only remained long enough to sight it in and get it "zeroed" and was back again in front that same night.

"Zeroing" a rifle is the process of testing it out on a range at known distances and setting the sights to suit one's individual peculiarities of aiming. Having once established the "zero" the marksman can always figure the necessary alterations for other ranges or changed conditions of wind and light.

From that time on, I "lived" in Sniper's Barn. It made no difference whether the battalion was in the front line or in billets, I was there for a purpose and I accomplished it. When the guns were in the front or in support, we had one mounted in the hedge and kept the rifle handy. Bouchard, with a large telescope, and I with my binoculars, scanned everything along the enemy's front and behind his lines. We knew the ranges, to an inch. If one or two men showed, I used the rifle; if a larger number, the machine gun.

Prior to this time, during all the very bad

weather, we had ample opportunities to shoot individual Germans from our Sniper's Barn position but had refrained because our own men were also necessarily exposing themselves daily, and to have started a sniping campaign would have done us no particular good and would certainly have resulted in additional deaths on our side. It seems that the troops opposed to us up to this time had been Saxons who were quite well satisfied to leave us alone provided we would do the same by them. Of course we did shoot them occasionally when they became too careless and exposed themselves in groups, but that was perfectly legitimate machine-gun work and taught them a well-needed lesson. Now, however, a different breed of Huns had come in and they had started the dirty work. They were Bavarians alternating with Marines, and we soon learned that for genuine low-down cussedness the Marine had them all beaten, although the Bavarians and Prussians were pretty bad.

When we first began on them it was no unusual occurrence to have from ten to twenty good open shots a day. The ranges averaged about six

hundred yards and as I was using a specially
targeted Ross rifle, equipped with the latest
Warner & Swazey sight, and as I had spent many
years in learning the finer points of military rifle
shooting, I am very much afraid that some of
them got hurt. For about a month we kept it up,
the "hunting" getting poorer every day until
finally the few German snipers working along the
front were safely ensconced in carefully prepared
dug-outs. A boche cap above the parapet was a
rare sight, but we had our hundred, all right;
and then some; for, as Bouchard said: "We'd
better get a little pay, in advance before they
'bump *us* off.'"

Several times in later days similar events occurred and in each case swift and terrible retri-
bution was meted out to the criminal enemy.
They shot down our stretcher-bearers, engaged
in their noble work of trying to save the wounded, but we took bloody toll from them whenever
this occurred, using unusual methods and taking
desperate chances, sometimes, to drive the lesson
home.

On one occasion our observers had reported

THE EMMA GEES

a large gathering of the enemy at a place called Hiele Farm, about eight hundred yards from our position and I had laid two guns on them when, through our telescope, I discovered that it was a burial party assembled in a little cemetery just behind the farm buildings and telephoned to the officer in charge that I did not intend to shoot up any funeral. Within a few minutes came word than an enemy sniper had shot and killed one of our most popular stretcher-bearers and had also fired several shots into the wounded man whom he was bringing in, killing him also. Then, without hesitation, I ordered both guns to open up and we maintained an intermittent fire on that place until long after dark. We could see numbers of Germans lying about on the ground. I have never regretted it.

Then, the day before Christmas, 1915, while the Twentieth Battalion was occupying the front line and we were back in the redoubts of the supporting line, I was up in the gun position at "S-P-7," the redoubt just in rear of the point where the slaughter of November twenty-seventh

had taken place, when a boche shell dropped
directly in the dug-out which was my home
when in the front line. It killed two men, one
I remember was named Galloway, and wounded
several others. I was so close that I could see
everything that happened. One of the wounded
was in such bad shape that the only possible
chance to save his life was to get him back
to a dressing station without delay. The communication trenches were washed out and the
only way was down that ill-fated Devil's Elbow
road. The officer in command called for volunteers to carry the man out, remarking that, as
it was Christmas Eve, he did not think
even a German would shoot at a wounded
man or unarmed stretcher-bearers. All hands
offered to go and two were chosen. The officer
went with them and they started down the road.
The minute they reached the fatal bend, where
they came in sight of the German lines, a shot
rang out and down went the first man. Another
shot and the second was down, while a third
dropped the officer, who was trying to assist the

fallen. I could see each shot strike in the water alongside the road and could tell just about the spot from whence they came so, although we had absolute orders never to fire from that position unless attacked, I immediately swung the gun around and commenced to "fan" that particular spot, at the same time calling to our signaler to get the Sixteenth Battery on the wire and call for S. O. S. fire. (Each yard of enemy line is covered by the guns of some one of our batteries which, when not firing, are kept "laid" on their particular section of parapet.) Within a few moments the battery opened up but not before at least a half dozen machine guns in our front line had been hoisted upon the parapets and were ripping Heinie's sand-bags across the way. During this proceeding the wounded men were recovered from the road, but, unfortunately, both the volunteer carriers and the man originally wounded had died. The officer, although painfully injured, recovered.

In retaliation for this trick, our heavy guns wiped out at least five hundred yards of German trench. It was the most artistic job of work I have ever seen. From a point approximately two hundred and fifty yards on either side of this murderer's nest we utterly destroyed every vestige of a parapet. How many of the assassins we killed will never be known, but our hearts were filled with unholy joy when we could distinguish bodies or parts of enemy's bodies among the debris thrown up by one of the big 9.2 shells.

CHAPTER X

A FINE DAY FOR MURDER

"SAY, kid, want to go sniping?" called out a lank individual as he came over the bridge at "S-P-7" one morning in December, 1915.

The person addressed, a swarthy little boy wearing the uniform and stripe of a lance-corporal of the Twenty-first Canadian Machine Gun Section, took a long careful look around the sky, hastily swallowed a strip of bacon he had in his fingers and as he darted into a little "rabbit-burrow" sort of tunnel, flung back the words; "Hell, yes; this looks like a fine day for a murder." In a few moments he reappeared with a water-bottle and a large chunk of bread. Hastily filling the former from a convenient petrol tin and cramming the latter into his pockets, he walked over to the older man and divested him of some of the paraphernalia with which he was festooned. He took a long case containing a tele-

A FINE DAY FOR MURDER

scope, another carrier holding the tripod, two
bandoliers of ammunition and a large haversack.

"How we going in?"

"Straight across," said the sniper.

"Ver-re-well, young-fella-me-lad, if you can
stand it I can," said the youngster, for he knew
full well that to go from there to Sniper's Barn
in broad daylight meant to expose himself to
observation from "Germany," only about five hundred yards away, and with a fat chance of playing
the part of "the sniper sniped."

Without another word they departed. The
sentry on guard at the crossing of the creek volunteered the cheerful hope that they'd get pinked
before they got across the field, upon which the
boy assured him that he would be drinking real
beer in London when the pessimistic sentry was
"pushing up the daisies" in Flanders. Crossing
the open field to a hedge, they slipped into a shallow remnant of an old French trench, just in time
to escape a snapping bullet which was aimed
about one second too late. From here they
crawled carefully along the hedge, bullets cutting

127

intermittently through the bare branches above them and, at last, came to a small opening that gave entrance to a garden, about one hundred yards from a group of demolished farm buildings. Here they rested for a few minutes, while the bullets continued to "fan" the hedge up which they had come and which led to the buildings.

The boy—"Bou" the other called him—worked his way along the ground to an old cherry tree and was about to lift up a sort of trap-door at its roots when the other stopped him.

"Never mind the gun," he said, "we'll just wait here until they do their morning strafe and then go into the buildings. I want to try for a few of them over on Piccadilly to-day and you can't use a machine gun for that. You'll simply have to be the observer, that's all."

Bou came back, lit a cigarette which the other promptly extinguished and then subsided.

"What you think you're going to do; shoot from the farm?" Bou couldn't possibly keep quiet any longer.

"Sure, Mike; why not?"

Canadian Soldiers in Action with Colt Machine Guns

A FINE DAY FOR MURDER

"Oh, nothing; but do you think we can get away with it?"

"Well, you've been here as long as I have and if you have not figured out the way the boches do things around this place I'm afraid I can't tell you; but I'll try. Now, they saw us come over here, didn't they? And they naturally think we are in the farm buildings. Just as soon as that fellow who was shooting at us can get word to their batteries they will proceed to shoot up the place. After about a dozen direct hits they will feel pretty well satisfied that they have either driven us out or 'na-pooed' us, so that will be our time to get inside and take a shot at this brilliant young Bavarian who will, without a doubt, be looking over the parapet in the hope that he may get a crack at us trying to 'beat it.' I've been wanting to get that guinea for a long time and have a hunch that this is our day. See?"

Before the boy could answer there came a swift "whit; whit; whit;" and three "bang; bang; bangs" in and above the main building of the farm. Followed several more salvos, finally

crashing through the walls and throwing up foun-
tains of brick-dust and earth. After waiting several minutes they worked their way carefully
along the hedge and around behind the buildings.
Entering the one nearest the road, which was a
mere shell with the roof and two walls entirely
gone, they crept cautiously across the floor, and
dodging the carcass of a cow that lay with its
head in an old fireplace, they finally found themselves in a back room. Many bales of tobacco
lay piled up on the floor, covered with the litter
and wreckage from the upper story. Here the
older man uncovered an opening under the tobacco, through which they entered a small chamber, perhaps eight feet square, comparatively
clean. At one side of this narrow space lay a
figure covered with the well-known blue overcoat
of the French soldier.

"Who's your friend?" inquired the youngster.

"I don't know; he was here when I first came;
but I think he was the original sniper of Sniper's
Barn. Look at that pile of shells beside him."

A FINE DAY FOR MURDER

Near the dead soldier was his rifle and a great pile of empty cartridge cases.

"We'll have to bury him some day: I think he earned it. He's got a hole right through the heart. Must have been here a year: he's all dried up, like a mummy."

While delivering this discourse the sniper had been carefully removing straw and tobacco leaves from an irregular hole in the brick wall. Here he set up the telescope and settled himself to scrutinize that part of the German line which lay directly opposite. After a few minutes' observation he began to clear away another and smaller opening, to the right of and below that where the telescope was set.

"He's there, all right: look just about four o'clock in the 'scope as it stands. See him, right beside that leaning tree? Keep your eye on him while I get my sight set."

In a few seconds, everything ready for action, the tall man sprawled himself on the floor, sling adjusted, piece loaded and cocked, while

Bou, now behind the telescope, whispered excited-
ly: "He's still there and looking right at me. I
can see his cap badge. He's one of those damned
Marines. Get him, Mac, for God's sake, get him,
quick."

"I'll get him, all right," muttered the other as
he gingerly poked the muzzle of his rifle through
the few remaining straws. "Now watch and see
if his hands come up and whether he falls forward or just drops;" with which he slowly pressed
the trigger and the shot roared in the small
chamber.

"You got him!" shrieked Bou; "I saw his hands
come up to his face and he pitched right forward into the trench. Hooray! that's another
one for Charlie Wendt."

CHAPTER XI

WITHOUT HOPE OF REWARD

ALL the bandsmen (we had both bagpipe and bugle bands) go into the front line with the other troops. They are unarmed, but equipped with first-aid kits and stretchers. It is their task to administer first aid to all wounded and then to carry or otherwise assist them back to the dressing stations which may be anywhere from a few hundred yards to a mile or more, depending on the ground. When a man is hit while in an exposed place, whether in No Man's Land or behind our lines, it is up to the stretcher-bearers to get to him at the earliest possible moment. I have seen these men, time after time, rush to the assistance of a stricken soldier, knowing full well that they would immediately become the target for snipers' bullets. Personal considerations never appeared to enter their heads. Never, in all my experience, have I seen one of them backward in going to the aid of a wounded man. Often they would spend hours in the effort to bring back to the lines some soldier too badly injured to help himself; and the pity of it was that, on many occasions, after all their self-sacrificing labor, they would be shot down just as they were about to come over the parapet and into the trench.

And all without hope of reward other than the love and admiration of their comrades. There was a time, before this war, when such exploits were considered worth the Victoria Cross. Now, however, they are merely a matter of daily routine. Thousands of men are, every day, performing deeds of valor, which in any other war would have brought the highest decorations, without receiving even so much as an honorable mention. Exposure to fire such as theorists had told us would demoralize any army is merely a part of the day's work. Troops go in and out of the trenches, often under artillery fire that, according to our books, ought to annihilate them, and they do it without thinking it anything unusual or worthy of comment other than perhaps, in answer to a question, to remark: "Oh, yes, they shot us up a bit in the P. & O." or "They handed us a few 'crumps' and 'woolly bears' coming through Ridgewood." ("Woolly bear" is the name given to a large, high explosive shell, with time fuse, which bursts overhead, giving out a dense black smoke, which expands and rolls about in such a manner as to suggest the animal for which it is named.) In fact, nearly all the names invented by the soldier to describe the various projectiles are so apt and expressive as to be self-explanatory. The "Silent Lizzies," "Sighing Susans" and "Whispering Willies" belong to the class of large caliber, long range naval gun shells which pass over the front line so high that only a sort of whispering sound is heard. The "middle heavies" with percussion fuses, which burst on impact and give out a dense black smoke, have been called "Jack Johnsons" and "coal boxes," but are now usually grouped under the general designation of "crumps," because of the peculiar sound of their explosion. They run

all the way from 4.1 inch to 9.2 inch calibers.
Some of the very large shells are called "Grand-
mothers" or "railroad trains." The French call
them "marmites," meaning a large cooking pot
or kettle. The "whizz-bang" is just exactly
what the name would suggest: a small shell of
very high velocity, which arrives and bursts with
such suddenness as to give no time for taking
cover. Its moral effect exceeds the material in
the trenches, but it is deadly along roads or in the
open. Gas shells have a peculiar sound, all their
own, difficult to describe but never forgotten
when once heard. It has been described as a
"rumbling" noise, but I think "gurgling" is better. (It's a pity some one can not take a phono-
graph into the lines and "can" some of these
things.) When gas shells land they do not make
much noise, having a very small bursting charge;
merely sufficient to break the case which contains
the gas in liquid form. They are often mistaken,
by new troops, for "duds" or "blinds," as we call
shells which fail to explode. As soon as the
liquid gas is liberated, however, it vaporizes and

British Machine Gun Squad Using Gas Masks

quickly spreads over a considerable area. There
are many kinds, but they can generally be distinguished by the smell. Some are merely lachry-
matory or "tear" shells; the gas affecting the
eyes in such a manner as to produce constant
"weeping" and consequent inability to see clear-
ly. Others, however, are deadly and one good
breath will put a man out of action and a couple
of "lungfuls" will usually kill him.

About this time, I think it was December 19th,
1915, we had our first experience with chlorine
gas or "cloud gas" as distinguished from "shell
gas." The troops on our immediate left got a
pretty bad dose, but, owing to the peculiar formation of the lines and varying air currents, we did
not suffer severely from it. The lines in the
Ypres salient were so crooked that the enemy
rarely attempted to use this form of gas after
the first big attack in April, 1915, as it
would frequently roll back upon his own troops.
Shell gas was constantly used, generally being
fired against our positions in the rear; artillery
emplacements and such. Being well equipped

THE EMMA GEES

with gas masks or respirators, we suffered little
harm from it.

Christmas, 1915, was a quiet day on our front,
both sides being apparently willing to "lay off"
for a day. There was no firing of any kind and
both our men and the enemy exposed themselves
with impunity. Aside from this, however, it was
the same as any other day. There was none of
the visiting and fraternizing of which we heard
so much on the previous Christmas. The Germans opposite us had a number of musical instruments and on that night and on New Year's Eve
they almost sang their Teutonic heads off.

January passed quietly. By this time we had
become so accustomed to the mud and rain that I
doubt if we would have been happy without them.
In spite of all the difficulties, we managed to get
our rations and *mail* every day. The regular
shelling had become a part of our daily life, and
the constantly growing list of killed and wounded
we accepted without comment. The Machine
Gun Section was gradually losing its original
members and replacing them by drafts from the

infantry companies. It was simply a case of "Conditions continue normal in the Ypres salient," to quote the official reports. We now maintained two strafing guns, shifting about from one position to another whenever an opportunity offered to harass the boche.

That winter, 1915-16, was what they call a "wet winter," that is, it rained continually and rarely got cold enough to freeze. With the exception of a light flurry in late November and a fairly heavy snow about the first of March, we never saw any of the "beautiful." A few times there was frost enough to make thin ice, but never enough to enable us to walk on top of the mud which was from six inches deep in the best parts of the trench to thigh deep in the worst. We had no rubber boots at the start but got some late in the winter.

A peculiar affliction, first noticed during this war, is what is known as "trench feet." Where men are required to remain for long periods standing in cold water and unable to move about to any great extent, the circulation of blood in the lower limbs becomes sluggish and, eventually, stops. The result appears to be exactly the same as that caused by severe frost-bite; in fact it *is* freezing without frost, (I don't know why not, if you can cook with a fireless cooker), and, in severe cases, amputation is necessary.

While the Imperial troops on our flank suffered considerably from this dreaded affliction, we had but few cases, although our position was infinitely worse than theirs, we being in lower ground. Probably the average Canadian is better able to stand the cold and wet than the native-born Briton. We had but one case in the Machine Gun Section and that was not severe.

As a preventive measure, whale oil was issued with positive orders that every man must, at some time during each twenty-four hours, remove his shoes and socks and rub his feet with this oil. I never did think the oil was anything but just an excuse to make the men rub as that in itself would be sufficient to restore the circulation. At any rate, when the oil gave out, we still kept up the rubbing game and there was no noticeable change in the result.

WITHOUT HOPE OF REWARD

Another hitherto unknown disease which developed during that season was what is commonly known as "trench fever." The victim's temperature runs up around one hundred and three and he is affected with lassitude and general debility and it requires from three weeks to a month in hospital to put him in shape for duty. The medical officers use a Greek name for this fever, which, translated, means, "a fever of unknown origin" but the colloquial designation is "G. O. K.," (God only knows). It is rarely, if ever, fatal. I never heard of any one dying of it.

Then there is a sort of skin affection; a "rash," which is said to be caused by eating so much meat, especially fats, without taking sufficient exercise. A few sulphur baths at specially prepared places behind the lines soon eradicate this trouble.

Really dangerous diseases are extremely rare. Typhoid fever is almost unknown, pneumonia is seldom heard of and even rheumatism, which one would naturally expect to be prevalent, is by no means common. The ratio of sickness, from all causes, was far below that in any of the training camps in this country although never, in Canada, England, Flanders or France, did we have as comfortable quarters as are furnished for all the troops here. But we *did* have at all times, plenty of good warm woolen clothing and an abundance of substantial food. Cotton uniforms, underwear or socks are unknown in any army except that of the United States. Perhaps you can find the answer in that statement.

During February an almost continuous fight was waged for a small length of trench on our left, known as the International Trench, because it changed hands so often. It culminated, March second, with the Battle of the Bluff, by which British troops took and held this line. We were in support, as usual, and suffered rather heavily from shell fire. This was the beginning of the spring offensive, and from that time on we caught it, hot and heavy, for four solid months.

CHAPTER XII

F ROM the time we first caught sight of our guns shelling the German airplanes there was rarely a day that we did not see many of them, scouting, bombarding or fighting. At first, as mentioned elsewhere, they flew very low; within easy range of machine-gun fire, but soon began to climb to higher altitudes until, at the time of my departure, most of their work was done from a height of about twelve thousand feet.

There was one of our planes, piloted by a major. I never heard his name but he was known all up and down the line as "The Mad Major." He was a pioneer in all the marvelous evolutions which now form an important part of the airman's training. Side slips, spinning dives, tail slides; all were alike to him. He would go over the enemy lines and circle about, directing the fire of a battery, scorning to notice the fire of the

143

THE EMMA GEES

"Archies," (flyers' name for anti-aircraft guns)
and when that job was finished, would come home
in a series of somersaults, loops and spins which
made one dizzy to watch. He was a great joker
and frequently, when the shell-bursts were unusually thick around him, would come tumbling
down from the sky like a shot pigeon, only to recover at a height of several hundred feet and
shoot off in a bee line for the airdome. I've
no doubt that the enemy often thought they had
"got him," but at last reports he was still there.

I watched the planes for months without seeing
one hit and had about concluded that, to make an
Irish bull, the only safe place on earth was up
in the air, when, one morning, hearing the now
familiar "put-put-put" of machine guns up above,
we looked up to see one of our large observing
biplanes engaged with a very small but fast enemy plane. The boche had all the best of it
and soon our plane was seen to slip and stag-
ger and begin to descend. The little "wasp"
came swooping down after it, firing all the while
until, when a few hundred feet from the ground,

German Aeroplane Trophy—Jules Vedrine Examining the Machine Gun

our machine turned its nose' straight downward
and crashed to earth, well behind our lines, both
occupants being instantly killed, or perhaps they
had already been killed by the bullets. The German thereupon turned and was soon back over his
own territory. That same afternoon, another of
our machines was shot down, apparently by the
same man, just opposite our position, inside the
German lines.

Shortly after this, when back in reserve, we
watched another fight directly over our heads.
This was a pitiful tragedy. One of England's best
and most famous flyers, Captain Saunders, had
been over the German lines and had engaged and
brought down an enemy and then, having
exhausted his ammunition, started back
"home" for more, but encountered a fast-flying
boche who immediately attacked him. Being
unable to return the fire, he tried every trick
known to the birdman to escape but without
avail. He came lower and lower in his evolutions
and finally settled into a wide and sweeping spiral. The boche did not come very low as several

machine guns and "Archies" opened on him. The other plane came slowly down in its perfect spiral course and, noticing that the engine was not running, we thought the aviator was intending to make a landing in a large open field toward which he was descending, but when the spiral continued until the tip of one wing touched the ground and crumpled up we knew there was something wrong and ran to the spot, not more than one hundred yards from where we were standing. We got the Captain out and found that he had been shot in the head but was still conscious. He died within a short time.

Other of our aviators who had witnessed his first fight furnished the beginning of the story and we could see that in the second engagement he never fired a shot, and every one of his magazines was empty. I examined them myself.

The large, sausage-shaped observation balloons sometimes afford a little diversion. When we were at Dranoutre one of them used to hang over our billeting place. One day an enterprising Hun came flying across and endeavored to attack it but was driven off by two of our planes.

Again, one of our balloons broke away in a strong wind and started toward Germany. Both the occupants of the basket made safe parachute descents with all their instruments and papers, but the balloon sailed swiftly away. Then the Germans opened on it with every gun in that sector. I feel sure that they fired at least two thousand shots at it. The air around was so filled with the smoke of shell-bursts that it was sometimes difficult to discern the balloon itself. It was late in the evening and the last we saw of the "sausage" it was still traveling eastward, apparently unhit. The joke of the whole thing is that the balloon was never hit and, the wind veering during the night, it returned and came down inside our lines within a few miles of its starting place.

On two occasions Zeppelins came over our lines, evidently returning from raids across the Channel. One time it was night and we could only hear, but not see the air-ship. The other time, during the St. Eloi fight, I saw one, just at daybreak. It was in plain sight but well over the German lines and headed east. No attempt was made to do any bombing of our positions by the Zeppelins although we occasionally received visits from bombing airplanes. The night before I left France, the last time, they dropped several bombs on the village of Ecoviers where I was staying. The only result was the killing of two civilians, the wounding of several others and the wrecking of one of the few whole houses in the town which had often been a victim of shells. Not a soldier was injured.

You have, no doubt, read of cases where bombs have been dropped on or near hospitals, ambulances and so on, and possibly you think that this was intentional on the part of the boche. If so you flatter him. This bomb dropping is, at best, very uncertain business and it would be well-nigh impossible for the most expert flyer to aim at and hit any single building. The fact is that, in nearly every town and city behind the lines, hospitals, ammunition stores and billets are located in close proximity to one another, with probably

a railway running near by, so that any attempt
to bomb the really important "military" points
will necessarily jeopardize the homes of non-
combatants—including hospitals. Even the Zeppelins, which are much more stable than an airplane, have never been able to place their bombs
with any degree of accuracy.

CHAPTER XIII

The Battle of St. Eloi

NO one realizes better than I the utter futility
of attempting to describe a modern battle
so that the reader can really understand or visual-
ize it. There are no words in any vocabulary that
convey the emotions and thoughts of persons during the long days and nights of horror—of the
continual crash of the shells, the melting away
or total annihilation of parapets and dug-outs;
being buried and spattered with mud and blood;
with dead and wounded everywhere and, worst
of all, the pitiful ravings of those whose nerves
have suddenly given way from shell shock. No
imagination can grasp it; no picture can more
than suggest a small part of it. None who has
not had the actual experience can ever understand it. The hospital and ambulance people
back at the rear see some of the results, but
even they can have no conception of what it is
like to be actually in the torment and hell-fire
at the front.

THE BATTLE OF ST. ELOI

I could not, if I so desired, give an accurate description of the operations in general. I have not the necessary data as to the various troops engaged or local results accomplished. Historians will record all that. My field of description is limited to my field of personal observation, which was not very extensive. I suppose, however, that I saw as much as it was possible for any one person to see, so I shall try to describe that part of the battle of St. Eloi in which it was my fortune to participate.

At the point at the southern end of the Ypres salient, where the line turns sharply to the eastward, stood the village of St. Eloi. It consisted of perhaps fifteen or twenty buildings of the substantial brick and iron construction characteristic of all Flemish towns and was situated at the intersection of the two main roads paved with granite blocks, one running to Ypres and the other through Voormezeele. The village itself, except for two or three outlying buildings, was inside our lines. The portion held by the enemy, however, included a prominent eminence, called the "Mound," which dominated our whole line for a mile or more. This mound had been a bone of contention for more than a year and several desperate attempts had been made to take it; notably in February and in March, 1915, when the Princess Pat's were so terribly cut up and lost their first Commanding Officer, Colonel Farquhar. All these attempts having failed, our engineers proceeded to drive tunnels and lay mines, six in number, so as to cut off the point of the German salient for a distance of about six hundred yards.

All was completed; mines loaded and ready, and the time for the attack was fixed for daybreak of the twenty-seventh of March. The mines were to be fired simultaneously, followed immediately by an attack, in force, by the Royal Fusiliers, the Northumberland Fusiliers and a battalion of the West Yorkshires. Our brigade (Fourth Canadian) was immediately to the right of the point of attack, but, as the Imperial troops had changed their machine guns for the lighter Lewis automatic rifles to be used with the advancing troops, it was deemed advisable to bring up all

ST. ELOI MAP

The map on the opposite page is known as St. Eloi map. It is particularly interesting as showing, very faintly, a great group of mine craters within the British lines. No. 1 *can be seen in the lower left section just above the horizontal fold in the map and to the left of the perpendicular.* Here the British line comes in at the lower left corner, where it almost immediately branches, passing through figures 44 and 77, joining the main line again at the left and below Shelley Farm. Within this loop are the six enormous mine craters. No. 2 is immediately to the right of figure 96, while 3, 4 and 5 are in a line with it just to the right of the perpendicular fold. The faint dotted line that comes to an apex just below St. Eloi is the British trench known as Queen Victoria Street. This map is made from air photographs dated March 5th, 1916.

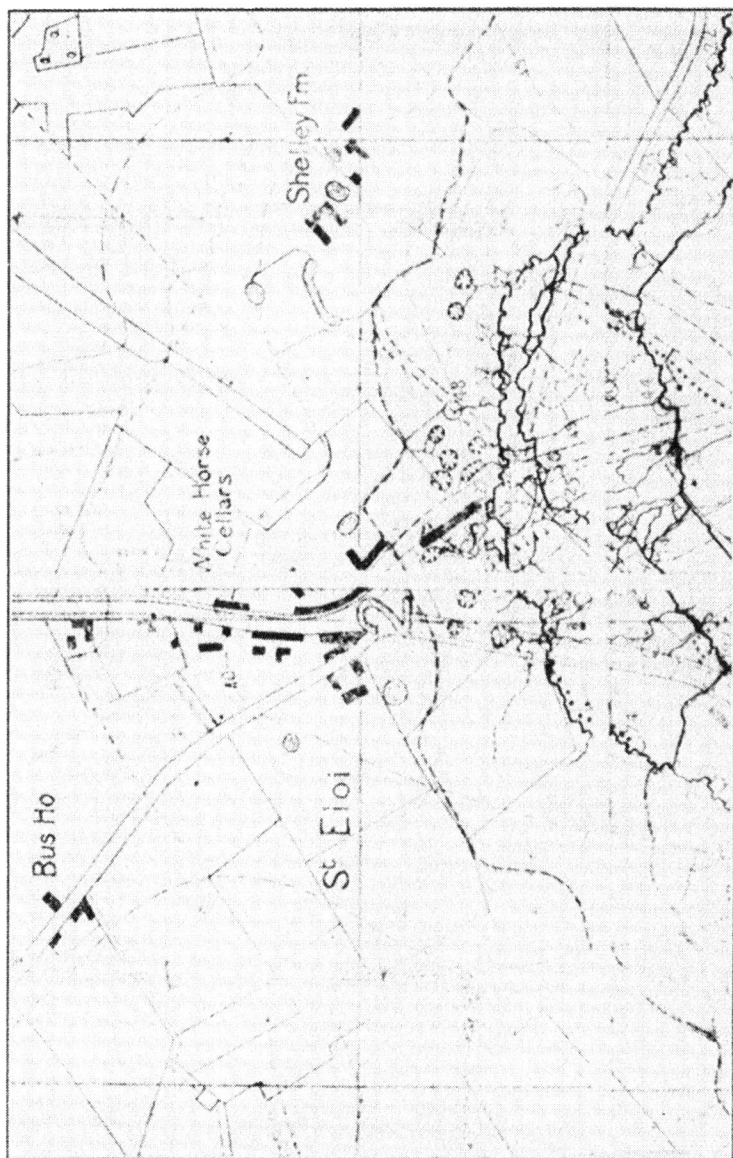

Bus Ho

White Horse
Cellars

St Eloi

Shelley Fm

170.

available machine guns of the heavier types to support the advance and to resist the inevitable counter-attacks. These guns, twelve in number, were
placed at advantageous positions on the flanks of
the attacking troops. I was only a sergeant at
that time, but, having been an officer, and having
had more actual experience in machine-gun work
than the others, the direct supervision of these
guns was entrusted to me.

We got all the guns up and in place during the
night of the twenty-sixth. In addition, our people
brought up a great many trench mortars of different calibers, with enormous quantities of ammunition. We then sat down to wait for the "zero"
hour, meaning the time for the show to begin.
I took my position at our extreme left, as I wanted
to be where I could see everything.

Promptly at the appointed time, the mines were
fired and then ensued the most appallingly mag-
nificent sight I have ever witnessed. There was
little noise but the very earth appeared to writhe
and tremble in agony. Then, slowly, it seemed
in the dim light, the ground heaved up and up

until, finally, bursting all bonds, earth, trees, buildings, trenches and men went skyward. Immediately followed great clouds of flaming gas, expanding and growing like gigantic red roses suddenly bursting into full bloom. It was an earthquake, followed by a volcanic eruption.

Before the flying debris had reached the ground the Fusiliers were over the top, fighting their way through the jungles of wire and shell craters. The occupation of the mine craters themselves was, of course, unopposed as there was no one there to offer opposition. They kept on, however, meeting the German reinforcements coming up from the rear, fighting them to a standstill and establishing themselves beyond the Mound.

Then all hell broke loose. From the beginning our artillery, machine guns and trench mortars had been maintaining a continuous fire, but the Germans, taken by surprise, were several minutes getting started. When they did open up, however, they gave us the greatest demonstration of accurate and unlimited artillery fire which I, or any of us, for that matter, had ever seen. The

air seemed to be literally full of shells bursting
like a million fire-flies. Our parapets were blown
down in a hundred places and the air was filled
with flying sand-bags, iron beams and timbers.
A shell struck under the gun by which I was
standing and flung gun, tripod, ammunition-box
and all, high into the air. Even under such conditions I could not help laughing at the ridiculous
sight of that gun as it spun around in the air,
with the legs of the tripod sticking stiffly out
and the belt of ammunition coiling and uncoiling
around it, like a serpent. The lance-corporal in
charge of it looked on, spell-bound, and when it
finally came down back of a dug-out, he looked
at me with a most peculiar expression and said:
"Well, what do you think of that?" Then he
jumped up and went after the wreckage and,
strange to relate, not a thing was broken. After
about twenty minutes of stripping and cleaning
he had the gun back on the parapet, shooting away
as though nothing had happened. He was an
Irishman, named Meeks.

I walked down the trench to get a spare barrel for a gun when a shell struck about ten feet in front, killing a man. I started on and another lit exactly where I had been standing. During that little trip of perhaps fifty yards and back I was knocked down and partly buried no less than four times.

Then the prisoners commenced to come back. They appeared to be glad to get out of it and I don't blame them. When they found that they had to go through the Canadian's lines, however, they held back. They had been told that the Canadians killed all prisoners. (We had heard something of the same kind about the Germans, too.) However, when our cooks came out with "dixies" full of steaming tea, with bread and marmalade sandwiches, they soon became reconciled. Our men made no distinction that morning between captor and captive, serving all alike with everything we had to eat or drink. At one time, however, owing to the congestion in the trench, we were compelled to "shoo" a lot of the prisoners back "overland," to the next support trench. As their artillery was raising

merry hell all over that section, they were a bit
backward about starting and it required threats
and a display of bayonets to get them out of the
trench and on their way. It was a funny sight
to see them beat it. There was little in the
way of obstacles to impede their progress and I
think that several of them came near to establishing new world's records for the distance. When
they arrived at the second line they wasted no time
in climbing down into it; they went in head-first,
like divers going into the water. I don't think
any of them was hit during this maneuver,
at least I did not see any of them fall.

Now, it has come to be an axiom that "any
one can take a trench but few can hold one."
It is another way of expressing the idea that
"it isn't the original cost—it's the upkeep."

It was no trick at all, with the assistance of
the mines, to advance our lines to what had been
the German third line, but, right there, some one
had made a miscalculation. It's a cinch our
"higher-ups" did not know how much artillery
the Germans had that they could turn on

that salient. Our own artillery had been greatly increased and they evidently thought we were at least equal to the enemy in this respect, but, say: the stuff he turned loose on us made our artillery look like pikers. For every "whizz-bang" we sent over he returned about a dozen 5.9's. By that night, nearly all the original attackers were gone and Fritz was back in at least two of the craters.

During the day a good many of us, including all our stretcher-bearers, made many trips through the devastated German trenches, getting out wounded and collecting arms and other plunder. I went up where the Fusiliers were trying to consolidate their position, intending to bring up a few guns if it appeared to be practicable, but abandoned the idea as, in my opinion, they were due to be shelled out within a short time, which proved to be correct. We did dig out and mount a German gun which was used for a while, but I then had it taken, with several others, back to our line. We could do so much more good from our original position by maintaining a con-

THE BATTLE OF ST. ELOI

tinuous barrage to hamper the enemy in getting up supports. From prisoners taken later we learned that our machine-gun barrage was much more effective than that of our artillery. However, as we were obliged to fire from temporary positions, on the parapet and without cover of any kind, it was impossible to prevent the loss of some guns by direct hits from shells. During that night and the next day a Highland brigade came up to relieve the Fusiliers. They included battalions of the Royal Scots and the Gordons.

By this time the Germans had brought up more guns and were keeping up such a terrific fire on our position that it did not seem humanly possible to hold it, but that night a bombing attack by the Fourth Canadian Brigade bombers, reinforced by about two hundred volunteers, retook the craters and reestablished our line in a more advanced position than that occupied by the original attackers. This line was thereafter called the Canadian trench to distinguish it from the other, which was called the British trench.

Early next morning we had a chance
to see some of the "Kilties" in action with
the bayonet, during a counter-attack, which they
repulsed. As I remember it, they did very little
shooting but jumped out of their trench to meet
the attackers with the cold steel. I never saw
any lot of soldiers who seemed so utterly determined to wipe out all opposition. They were
like wild men; savage and blood-thirsty in the
onslaught and, although the Germans must have
outnumbered them at least three to one, they never
had a chance against those brawny Scots. But
few of the boches got back to their own line and
no prisoners were taken. We then appreciated the
nickname given by the Germans (first applied to
Canadian Highlanders at Langemarck, but afterward used to designate all "Kilties"), "The Ladies
from Hell."

From that time the Canadians were alone in
the fight. The Fusiliers, having started it, faded
away, and the Scots, after a few brief days, likewise vanished and for two months or more St.
Eloi was a continuous struggle between the Sec-

ond Canadian Division and at least four German Divisions, including some of the infamous Prussian Guards.

During the next twelve days the fighting was almost uninterrupted. Troops came in and troops went out, but the Emma Gees held on, forever, as it seemed to us. But few remained of the original gun crews who started the engagement. Not all had been killed or wounded, but it had been necessary to relieve some who were utterly exhausted. How I kept going is a mystery to me as it was to others at the time. One thing which probably helped was the fact that I never, for one minute, permitted myself to think of anything except the matter of keeping those guns going. Sentiment I absolutely cast out. I was nothing but a cold-blooded machine. Good friends were killed but I gave them no thought other than to get the bodies out of the trench so that we need not step on them. To tie up and assist wounded was a mere matter of routine. In no other way could I have withstood the awful strain. I was hit, slightly, on several occasions but never severely enough to necessitate my going out. A dug-out in which I had a table where I wrote reports and figured firing data was hit no less than three times while I was in it, finally becoming a total wreck. The fact that I was not killed a hundred times was due to just that many miracles—nothing less. My leather jacket and my tunic were cut to shreds by bits of shell, a bullet went through my cap and another grazed my head so close as to raise a red welt, but that same old "luck" which had become proverbial in the battalion, still held and I was not seriously injured.

Our troubles were not all caused by artillery fire by any means. Fritz had a large and varied assortment of "Minenwerfer" with which to entertain us at all hours, day and night. A good many people, even among the soldiers themselves, think that Minenwerfer or "Minnie" for short, is the name of the projectile or torpedo, while, as a matter of fact, it is the instrument which throws it; a literal translation being "mine-thrower." In the same way they often speak of

THE BATTLE OF ST. ELOI

the shells thrown by trench mortars as "trench mortars" themselves. Now the family of "Minnies" is a large one and includes every device, from the ancient types used by the Greeks and Romans, with springs of wood, to the latest and most modern contraption in which the propelling power may be steel springs, compressed air or a small charge of powder. In its smallest form it is simply a "rifle grenade," somewhat similar to a hand grenade or ordinary "bomb," to which is attached a rod of brass or iron which slips down into the bore of the regular service rifle and is fired with a blank cartridge. Other and newer types are without this rod but have vanes or rudders affixed to the rear end which serve to guide the projectile in its flight. These usually have a hole through the center through which the bullet passes and can thus be used with the regular service ammunition. This whole class, embracing everything from the small "pineapples," fired from the rifle, to the monstrous "aerial torpedoes," are commonly spoken of as "fish-tails."

The shells from the trench mortars proper,

163

and most of the "fish-tail" family, are somewhat similar to ordinary artillery shells in that they are made of steel or iron and designed to burst into small fragments, each of which constitutes a deadly missile. On the other hand, the "mines" thrown by the Minenwerfer, are merely light sheet-metal containers for heavy charges of high explosives (T. N. T. or tri-nitro-toluol as a rule), and depend for their effectiveness on the shock and blasting effect of the detonation. They have been increasing in size continually. At first we called them "sausages," then "rum-jars" (they resembled the ordinary one-gallon rum jar in size and shape), then they became "flying pigs" and by this time, I have no doubt, new and still more expressive names have been applied to them.

The havoc created in a trench by one of the large ones passes belief. The strongest dug-out is wiped out in a twinkle; whole sections of parapet are obliterated, and where was a strong, well-built wall eight feet or more in height there remains a hole or "crater" fifteen or twenty feet in diameter and several feet deep. Any man who happens to be within this area is, of course, blown to atoms, while frequently men in the near vicinity, but not exposed to the direct blast, are killed instantaneously by the shock. Medical men say that the effect is identical to that known as "caisson sickness," and is caused by the formation of bubbles of carbonic acid gas in the blood vessels. Not being a "medico" I can not vouch for this, but you can take it for what it is worth.

In daylight it is not difficult to dodge these devilish things and even at night, if they come one at a time, it is possible to escape the most of them, but when they come over in flocks, as they sometimes do, it is more a matter of luck than anything else.

CHAPTER XIV

FOURTEEN DAYS' FIGHTING

BY this time there was no doubt of the enemy's superiority in artillery, and to make matters worse, the craters were changing hands daily or even hourly. We never knew, for sure, whether our troops or those of the enemy held any certain crater, except the ones on each end, numbers one and six (we held them throughout the entire two months of fighting), but numbers two, three, four and five were debatable ground for several weeks. On two occasions I made the complete circuit of all the craters at night, going through the Canadian trench and coming back via what had been our original front line. On one of these trips I was accompanied by Captain Congreve, afterward Major Congreve, V. C., (now dead) who was the only staff officer I saw in that sector during all the time we were in the line. Sometimes we met individual

166

Lewis Gun in Action in Front-Line Trench

FOURTEEN DAYS' FIGHTING

German sentries and quick, quiet and accurate work was necessary to avoid detection and probable capture. I found that a French bayonet, the rapier shape, was a very satisfactory weapon at such times. Trench knives have been invented since and may be an improvement. After leaving me that night Captain Congreve came upon a party of eighty-two Germans, commanded by an officer, who had been cut off in one of the craters for several days, without food or ammunition, and captured them all, single-handed. For this feat he received the Distinguished Service Order and promotion to Major. Later, on the Somme, he continued his brilliant work and won the award of the Victoria Cross, but was killed at Mametz Wood before receiving the decoration, which was given to his widow. He was only twenty-five at the time of his death but had proved himself one of the most enterprising officers in the British army.

What had been left of the village of St. Eloi when the fight commenced was rapidly disappearing under the hail of shells. Where our original front line had been there remained but few detached fragments of parapet. For perhaps six hundred yards we were holding on with scattered and isolated groups. At one place, on our immediate left, was a hole in the line at least two hundred yards wide. Time after time the Canadians attacked and retook the craters, only to be literally blown out of them by the ensuing hurricane of shells.

The task of getting out the wounded was heart-breaking. Our own stretcher-bearers worked night and day, but they had suffered many casualties and were unequal to the task. The Border Regiment and the Durham Light Infantry, who occupied our old trenches and were not under heavy fire, sent volunteer carrying parties to assist in the work, so that all were taken out with a minimum of delay. It was impossible to remove the dead and they were buried in shell-holes, where they fell. During the succeeding days many were disinterred by other shells.

Then, the matter of maintaining communication with our supports and the headquarters in the rear was of the utmost importance and our signalers waged a continuous fight, against heavy odds, to keep the wires connected up. It would not be fair to others to specify any particular branch as being better. All who serve in the front line at a time like this are equally entitled to credit. At times, when it is necessary to go out and search for breaks and repair them, the work of the signalers is "extra hazardous," just as is that of the stretcher-bearers when obliged to expose themselves to succor the wounded, or the machine gunner when it is necessary to mount his gun on top of the parapet, within plain sight of the enemy, or the riflemen, bombers and scouts in advancing to the attack. There can be no fair distinction—they all, taken as a unit, are in a class separated by a wide gulf from those back in supporting or reserve or artillery positions, who, in turn, are separated from the transport and ambulance drivers, who, while occasionally under shell fire, are in the zone of comparative safety, where "people" still live and farm and run stores and estaminets. I would not have you think that I am minimizing the value of the services of these men. Their work is of vital importance to the success of the fighting forces and *must* be done; and I can truly say that in all my experience I have never known them to fail in the performance of their duties.

In this war, as in most others, it is the infantry-man who stands the brunt of the fighting. True, he is disguised under many other names, such as rifleman, bomber, automatic rifleman, rifle-grenadier, scout, signaler, sniper, runner or machine gunner but, when you get right down to the bottom of the whole business, he is the fellow who travels on his two feet and actually "goes over and gets 'em." Trenches can be battered to pieces by artillery but they can not be actually "taken" and held by any one but the plodding, patient, long-suffering "doughboy" or "web-foot" as he is called by the men of the other branches.

At one time, during this period, Sergeant H. Norton-Taylor and four men from our section, held one of the craters for five days, against numerous attacks, and even captured prisoners. They had no food, water or ammunition other than that which they could get from the bodies of dead·soldiers in the immediate vicinity. We sent many detachments to relieve them but were unable to locate their position and it was only by accident that they were discovered and relieved by a scouting party of the Nineteenth Battalion which was over on our left. But for this, they might be there now, as they were not the quitting kind.

Norton-Taylor was commissioned and commanded the section at Courcellette, where he was killed, September 15, 1916. He came of a long line of distinguished British officers, his father having been a Colonel in the Royal Field Artillery. A brother and a brother-in-law were in the service, one of them losing both feet by a shell. A sister was working in the hospitals in France and another in England. He was a true friend and a gallant officer—every inch a gentleman.

On the night of April tenth we were relieved by the Twentieth Battalion and went out for a

rest. I had not laid down to sleep for fourteen
days, snatching what rest I could, for fifteen
or twenty minutes at a time, leaning against a
parapet or propped up in the corner of a traverse.
We were only able to get as far as Voormezeele,
where we stopped in the ruins of the convent
school, and dropping on the stone floor slept
like the dead for twenty-four hours. The place
was being shelled all this time but none knew
or cared. The next night we made our way to
where the battalion was in billets, near Renning-
helst, where I immediately "flopped" for a
straight forty-eight hours' continuous sleep.
After that a bath, a shave and general clean-up,
supplemented by a good hot "feed," made me as
good as new. During that two weeks up in front
we had had no warm food, nothing but "bully
and biscuits" and, occasionally, a can of "Macono-
chie," a ration of prepared meat and vegetables,
which is excellent when served hot but not very
palatable when eaten cold.

We now had the longest rest we had enjoyed
since coming over, as we did not go back to the

FOURTEEN DAYS' FIGHTING

front line until April twentieth. Our Sixth and Fifth Brigades had been in during the time we were out and both had suffered severely in the many counter-attacks, but held on, like true British bull-dogs, to what had been our original front line. The craters were lost as it was impossible for any troops to hold them under the devastating fire of the German guns. Nearly every battalion of the Second Canadian Division had retaken one or more of them but, as it only resulted in additional loss of life, it was decided by the higher command to give it up and endeavor to re-establish our front along its original line.

We went in via Voormezeele, a town of several thousand inhabitants before the war, now a pile of ruins. From here a *pavé* road ran directly to St. Eloi and there had been two good communication trenches leading up to the front line. We soon discovered however that several things had happened during our absence. On the road to St. Eloi and about five hundred yards behind our front line, had been a Belgian farm called Bus House. (A London omnibus was lying, smashed,

in front of it.)   This place was now but a pile
of brick and timbers.   To the left, another group
of farm buildings, called Shelley Farm, was in
about the same condition, and where St. Eloi had
been was nothing but a barren waste.   Not a sign
of a house or any part of a house was visible;
not a brick remained and even the roads, the fine
stone-paved roads, had been obliterated.   Where
had been hedges or trees there was nothing but
a desolate expanse of mud which, from a distance,
appeared to be a smooth level plain.   For a good
six hundred yards back of our front line there
was not a shrub or bush or tree nor any land-
mark of any kind.   Every inch of this ground
had been churned over and over again by shells.
Literally, it was not possible to set foot on a
spot which had not been upturned.   The whole
area was simply a continuation of shell craters,
joined and interlocked without a break.   Where
our communication and support trenches had
been it was just the same.   No man could have
gone over that ground and said: "Here was a
house," or "There was a field," or "That was once

FOURTEEN DAYS' FIGHTING

a road," because house, turnip field and road looked exactly alike. The great granite blocks of the road had been pulverized to dust, and the bricks of the houses had shared a like fate. Even the contour of the ground was changed—ditches, depressions and ridges having been hammered to a uniform elevation.

And every hole was full of water. To traverse this desert one must wade and flounder through liquid mud waist deep and sometimes deeper. Yet it had to be done. We had nine positions up there at each of which a handful of men must be relieved daily; or rather nightly, as it was, obviously, impossible to move about over that open expanse in daylight. Every yard of it was under scrutiny from the German lines and, even at night, owing to the lavish use of star-shells by the enemy, it was a long and slow journey as it was necessary to stop and remain absolutely quiet when a light came near.

The hardest thing about the whole business was to find the men who were to be relieved. There was no path nor road nor land-mark of any kind. During the time we were in, it rained continuously and at no time was a star visible. The positions where they were stationed were exactly like the rest of the surrounding country— merely enlarged shell-holes with, perhaps, a frag- ment of a sand-bag parapet. No lights could be shown, they did not even dare use "Very lights," as our "star-lights" are known. They were not in any regular formation but at irregular inter- vals along what had been a very crooked line. Fortunately, we had a "natural born" guide on our first trip in and we found them all. After that we managed to "carry on" but not without many slips. It was nothing unusual for a relief party suddenly to find themselves in the German lines and have to work their way out as best they could. If caught out after dawn one had to lie low in a shell-hole all day, probably under heavy artillery fire, until darkness came and made it possible to return unseen. This trouble was not confined to our side and it was by no means an uncommon occurrence for parties of the enemy to get lost in the same way. Some-

Canadian Machine Gunners Digging Themselves Into Shell-Holes

times these adventures resulted in rather sharp
bombing engagements. One night a whole
platoon of about forty Germans went through
a gap in our line and bumped into a strong supporting party of ours at Shelley Farm where they
were all captured. They had been looking for
one of the craters whose garrison they were to
relieve. Individual prisoners were taken nearly
every night.

Under the prevailing conditions, it was impossible to take machine guns up, so we depended
entirely upon Lewis guns. Fortunately no determined attack was made on us during this time
as it is extremely doubtful if we could have held
them there. We would, of course, have stopped
them a few hundred yards back, at our support
line, and I must confess that I had at times a
sneaking desire to see them come over and
get into that mud so we could move back to
comparatively comfortable quarters.

As we no longer had any trenches, we
abandoned the old letter method of designation
and simply numbered the various positions. On

the first morning in, the gun and crew at No. 14 were blown up by a shell. This was an unlucky position as the same thing had happened there to a crew from the Twentieth Battalion. We then moved that position some fifty yards to one side and had no further trouble.

We alternated with other battalions of the division, going in and out, holding that line and gradually improving it, until, on the twenty-second day of May, while we were back in billets, I was "warned for leave" (a week in England), and little Bouchard, my particular protégé and warmest friend, was to go along.

You people who have stayed at home can never realize what "leave" means to a soldier after eight months in the trenches and I, for one, will not attempt the impossible by trying to describe the sensation.

We packed our kits and hiked to Poperinghe, where, after sitting up all night, we took train at four o'clock A. M., arriving at Boulogne about noon and were in "Blighty" by four in the afternoon.

"Oh, ain't it a grand and glorious feeling!"

CHAPTER XV

BLIGHTY AND BACK

IN London we found things running along about as usual and proceeded to enjoy ourselves. Oh, the luxury of having clean clothes and being able to keep them clean; to sleep in real beds and eat from regular dishes and at white-clothed tables. It seemed almost worth the price we had paid to be able to get so much downright enjoyment out of the merest "necessities" of ordinary civilian life. The theaters were all running and we took in some show every night, but I derived the most satisfaction from taking my young companion around to see the museums and many old historical places in and about London. He was a stranger and I was fairly well acquainted.

But, when the time drew near for us to go back, I began to experience a feeling of depression. While I had not noticed it before, I suppose the

cumulative effect of the experiences of the last
eight months was beginning to tell on me. ˝ I
noticed that Bouchard appeared to be in about
the same condition. He would sometimes sit for
an hour or more, in our room at the Cecil, gazing
into space, never uttering a word. Poor
boy, while of course he could not *know* that this
was to be his last trip, I believe he had a presenti-
ment that such was the case.

I found myself now and then "checking up" my
own physical and mental condition. I had been
slightly injured several times—two scratches from
bullets on my left hand, a bullet in my right elbow,
two pieces of shell in my shoulder, a knee-cap
knocked loose and a fractured cheek-bone
from the fuse-cap of a "whizz-bang." None
of these had put me out of action for more
than a few hours and I had managed to keep
out of the hospital. (I had an instinctive dread
of hospitals.) But I knew, right down in my
heart, that my nerve was weakening. Thinking
over some of the things we had done, I believed
I could never do them again. I do not think

the man ever lived who would not, eventually, get into this condition. Some men "break" at the first shell that strikes near them, while others will go for months under the heaviest shell fire but, as I have said, it will certainly get them in the end. Of course I did not express any of these feelings to Bouchard, but tried to keep things moving all the time so as to give him little opportunity to worry. But, to tell the truth, I guess I needed the diversion more than he did, for he was the bravest and "gamest" youngster I ever knew.

Before we left France for our week in London I was told by my Colonel that I had been recommended for a commission and something or other in the way of a decoration and he suggested that I call upon General Carson, Canadian General in London, and find out about it. I did call at the General's office several times but was unable to see him. It afterward developed that the commission had already been gazetted and I was really and truly a First "Leftenant." I did not hear of it for nearly a month and, during the interval, went through, as a sergeant, one of the hottest times in my whole career.

When our leave was up we, together with hundreds of others, left Victoria Station early one morning for Folkestone and Boulogne and so on, back to Poperinghe, where we arrived just at daybreak the following morning and were welcomed by an early rising boche airman, who dropped about half a dozen bombs, evidently aimed at the railroad station. Fortunately, no one was hit. Then we trudged down the road, kilometer after kilometer, every one gloomy and grouchy, looking for our several units. Ours had moved and we spent the whole day before we located it.

We found the battalion in camp near the town of Dickebusch and soon settled down to the same old routine. They had not been back in the line since we left but had been engaged in some special work in and around this town, about which there is an interesting story.

Dickebusch was a town of several thousand inhabitants and considerable commercial importance, located on the Ypres-Bailleul road, about three and one-half miles directly west of St. Eloi. All troops going into the line anywhere from Wytschaete to Hill 60 were obliged to pass through or very close to it. Just east of the town was a shallow lake or pond, about a mile long and half as broad, called Dickebusch Etang, to cross which it was necessary to follow a narrow causeway, constructed by our engineers. While we continually passed and repassed through the place, we never had any troops actually billeted there, as it was within easy range of the German guns and was still occupied by the native population.

About the time of the St. Eloi affair, however, one of our Brigade Headquarters had been located in a group of buildings at the edge of the town, perfectly camouflaged and concealed from aircraft observation. It had long been suspected that there were spies among the people of this place and that they had effective means of communicating with the enemy, so when Fritz turned his guns on that headquarters, no one was very much surprised, but a determined effort was made to discover the guilty parties. Just what means were used I do not know, but it was learned that several of the prominent citizens, including the mayor or burgomaster, were in on it and they were summarily dealt with.

Following this, German airmen dropped notices into the town, warning all the civilians to get out as they were going to raze it to the ground. Not many would have gone, however, had not our authorities ordered the evacuation. As soon as the people had moved out, our troops proceeded to prepare the buildings for use as billets, reinforcing lower rooms and cellars with iron beams and protecting them with sand-bags. This was the work with which our battalion, and others, had been occupied and was just about completed when, true to their word, the Heinies started in, systematically, to write "finis" for Dickebusch. The church had already been pretty well shot up, as well as the surrounding graveyard where many of the tombs and monuments were smashed and the dead thrown from their graves. This blowing up of the dead seems to be a favorite pastime with the gentle Hun. They, the Germans, were now engaged in the demolition of the buildings along the principal streets and were doing it in a very thorough manner. We had here many demonstrations of a matter about which I have been questioned, times without number, by both military men and civilians, and that is, "What is the effective radius of a shell of a certain caliber?" It is one of the things which our theorists in general, and artillerymen in particular, delight in. Many hours of learned discourse have been devoted to proving, theoretically, that an area of a given size can be made impassable by dropping a certain number of shells on it, at stated intervals. This is all rot. Common sense should teach us better. The plain fact is that it depends entirely upon what the shell strikes. If it falls on soft earth, the effect is merely local and a man within a few feet would be uninjured; while, should it fall on a hard, stone-paved road, pieces might be effective at a distance of half a mile or more.

THE EMMA GEES

In the bombing schools we are told that the Mills hand grenade has an effective radius of ten yards, yet one will quite frequently escape unhurt from a dozen of them bursting within this radius and yet may be hit by a fragment from a distance of two hundred yards or more. All these theories are based on the assumption that the ground on a battle-field is level, free from obstructions and of a uniform degree of hardness; not one of which conditions ever exists. A small ditch, a log or stump or a water-filled shell-hole will make so much difference in the effect of the explosion of a shell or bomb that all efforts to prove anything by mathematics is a waste of time. If one is unlucky he will probably get hurt, otherwise not.

CHAPTER XVI

OUT IN FRONT FIGHTING

WE had been "home" but a few days when we received rush orders to pack up and march toward Ypres. There had been an intense bombardment going on up that way and we soon learned the cause from straggling wounded whom we met coming along the road. It was the second of June, 1916, and the Germans had launched their great surprise attack against the Canadians at Hooge. It was the beginning of what has been called the Third Battle of Ypres, but will probably be recorded in history as the Battle of Sanctuary Wood.

The enemy had gradually increased his customary bombardment and then, assisted by some mines, had swept forward, in broad daylight, overwhelming the defenders of the first and second lines by sheer force of numbers and had only been checked after he had driven through our

187

lines to a depth of at least seven hundred yards over a front of nearly a mile, including the village of Hooge, and was firmly established in a large forest called Sanctuary Wood and in other woods to the south. By the time we had arrived at our reserve lines (called the G. H. Q. or General Headquarters Line), we were diverted and directed to a position on the line just south of the center of the disturbance where we "dug ourselves in" and held on for four days. Shell fire was about all we got here, but there was plenty of that. The rifle and machine-gun bullets that came our way were not numerous enough to cause any concern although we did lose a few men in that way.

Here the news of the fight filtered through to us. It seemed that the Princess Pat's (unfortunate beggars), had got another cutting-up, together with some of the Mounted Rifles, and Major-General Mercer and Brigadier-General Victor Williams, who had been up in the front line on a tour of inspection, had both been wounded and captured. General Mercer after-

188

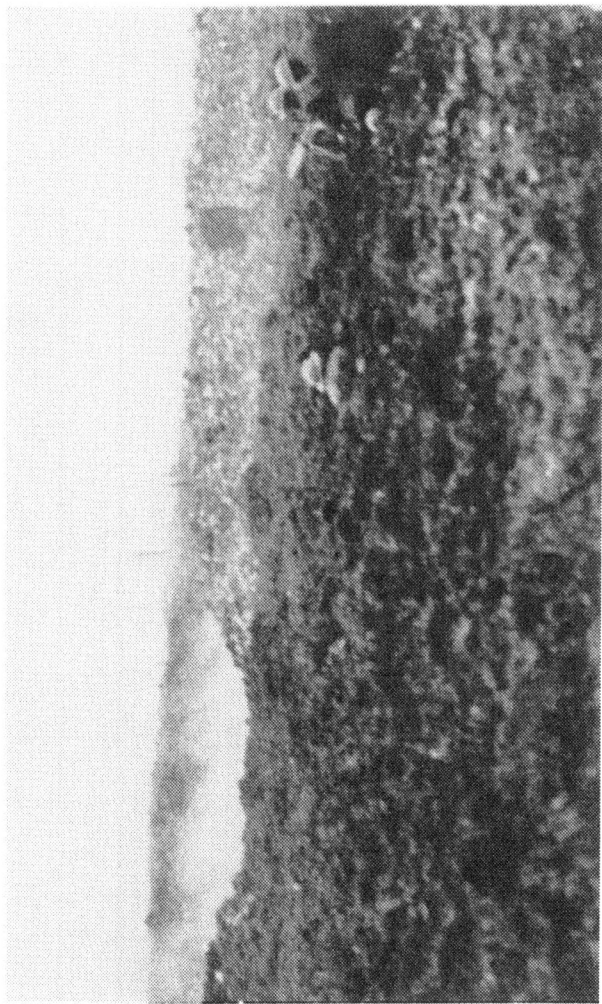

A Shell Exploding in Front of a Dug-in Machine Gun

OUT IN FRONT FIGHTING

ward died, in German hands, but General
Williams recovered and remains a prisoner. It
was said that less than one hundred from each
the Pat's and the Fourth C. M. R. came out
of the fight.

At this place several of our gun positions were
in the grounds of what had been one of the most
beautiful châteaux in Flanders—the Château
Segard, hundreds of years old but kept up in
the most modern style until the war came. Now
the buildings were but a mass of ruins. Not only
this but the grounds had been wonderfully laid
out in groves, gardens, moats and fish-ponds with
carefully planned walks and drives throughout
the whole estate which comprised at least forty
acres. There were trees and plants from all over
the world; beautiful borders and hedges of sweet-
smelling, flowering shrubs and cunningly planned
paths through the thickets, ending at some old
wondrously carved stone bench with perhaps an
arbor covered with climbing rose bushes.

All had felt the blighting touch of the vandal
shells. The trees were shattered, the roads and

paths torn up, the ponds filled with debris and the beautiful lawn pitted with craters, but in spite of all this devastation, the flowers and trees were making a brave fight to live. I could not but think, as I wandered through this place, how well the little flowers and the mighty oaks typified the spirit of France and Belgium. Sorely stricken they were—wounded unto death; but with that sublime courage and determination which have been the admiration of the world they were resolved that *they should not die.*

Along the main road leading up to the château was a charming little chapel, handsomely decorated and appointed. It was the only structure on the estate that had not been struck by a shell. We used it as sleeping quarters for two crews whose guns were located in the immediate vicinity. One night a big shell struck so close as to jar all the saints and apostles from their niches and send them crashing to the floor, but did no other damage.

This same thing happened to us once when we were sleeping in the convent school at Voormezeele, when all the statues on the walls were hurled down upon us by a large shell which struck the building.

The boys used to take these sacred effigies and place them on graves of their dead friends. We were not a very religious bunch but I suppose they thought it might help some—at any rate it proved their good intentions and I never interfered to stop it.

For several days the fighting continued furiously, the Canadians recovering some of the lost ground, including most of Sanctuary Wood, and then things settled down to the old "siege operation." During this time we had many opportunities to watch the splendid work of the men of the ammunition columns taking shells up to the batteries in broad daylight and within plain view of the enemy lines. It was one of the most inspiring sights I have ever witnessed and brought back memories of pictures I had seen of artillery going into action in the old days.

Down the road they would come, on the dead gallop, drivers standing in their stirrups, waving their whips and shouting at the horses, while the limbers bounded crazily over the shell-torn road, the men holding on for dear life and the shells bursting with a continuous roar all about them. It was the sight of a lifetime, and whenever they came past our men would spring out of the trenches and cheer as though mad. Time after time they made the trip and the escapes of some were miraculous. A few were hit, wagons smashed and horses and men killed or wounded, but not many, considering the number of chances they took.

The stories of heroism during that first day's fighting equal anything in history. Batteries were shot down to a man but continued working the guns to the last. One artilleryman, the last of his gun squad, after having one arm shot off at the elbow, continued to load and fire. Then a shell blew off about a foot of the muzzle of the gun but he still kept it going. He was found, lying dead across his gun and a trail of clotted blood showed where he had gone back and forth to the ammunition recess, bringing up shells. One member of the crew remained alive long enough to tell the story.

In another place, in Sanctuary Wood, were two guns known as "sacrifice guns," as they were intended to cover a certain exposed approach in case of an attack and to fight to the finish. How well they carried out their orders may be judged from the fact that every man was killed at the guns, *by German bayonets,* after having shot down many times their own number of the enemy.

Our old friends of the Lahore Battery lost so many men that they were having difficulty in maintaining an effective fire until two of our machine-gun squads volunteered to act as ammunition carriers, which they did for several hours, suffering heavy casualties.

Here occurred the only case of which I have ever heard where one of our medical officers was apparently "murdered." Captain Haight, M. O. of one of our western battalions was reported, on excellent authority, to have been bayoneted and. killed while attending the wounded.

While we were here, Major-General Turner,

THE EMMA GEES

V. C., who was in command of the entire Canadian Corps, paid us a visit. He came up unannounced and accompanied by a lone Staff Captain. I was instructed to act as his guide over our sector. During one trip along an exposed road we found ourselves in the midst of a furious hail of shells. I looked at the General to see if he wanted to take cover (I'm sure the rest of us did); he never "batted an eye" but continued at an even pace, talking, asking questions and stopping here and there to observe some particular point. I overheard one of our men say: *"General* Turner? General *Hell!* he ain't no general; *he's* a reg'lar *soldier."*

On the night of the sixth we were relieved and, next day, took up our quarters in Dickebusch. The Emma Gees had taken possession of a bank building, about the best in town, and had strengthened it, inside and out, with steel and sand-bags until it looked as though it would withstand any bombardment. Fortunately it was not hit while we were there, although many large shells fell very near; but when I again passed that

HOLLEBEKE TRENCH MAP

The map on the opposite page is a reproduction of what is known as "Hollebeke Trench Map— Part of Sheet 28." Famous Hill 60 is shown encircled by a contour line, just below Zwarteleen. The road running off at top and left of map leads to Ypres. The black and white line immediately to the right of this army road is the railroad from Ypres to Comines. The fine irregular lines represent the perfect network of main and communication German trenches. Various signs indicate supply dumps, dug-outs, mine craters, observation posts, earthworks, mine craters fortified, hedges, fences or ditches, churches, mills, roads, footpaths, entanglements, ground cut up by artillery fire, etc., etc. The British front-line trench is shown very faintly on this reproduction but can be picked up as it passes through the first "e" in Zwarteleen and traced up past the figure 30. At the left of Zwarteleen it can be seen crossing the railroad and army road. This map, as were the others, was carried by Captain McBride and the section shown represents about one-sixth of the total size. It was made from photographs taken by Allied aviators. The blurred line bisecting the map just below figures 35 and 36 is one of the well worn folds in the map.

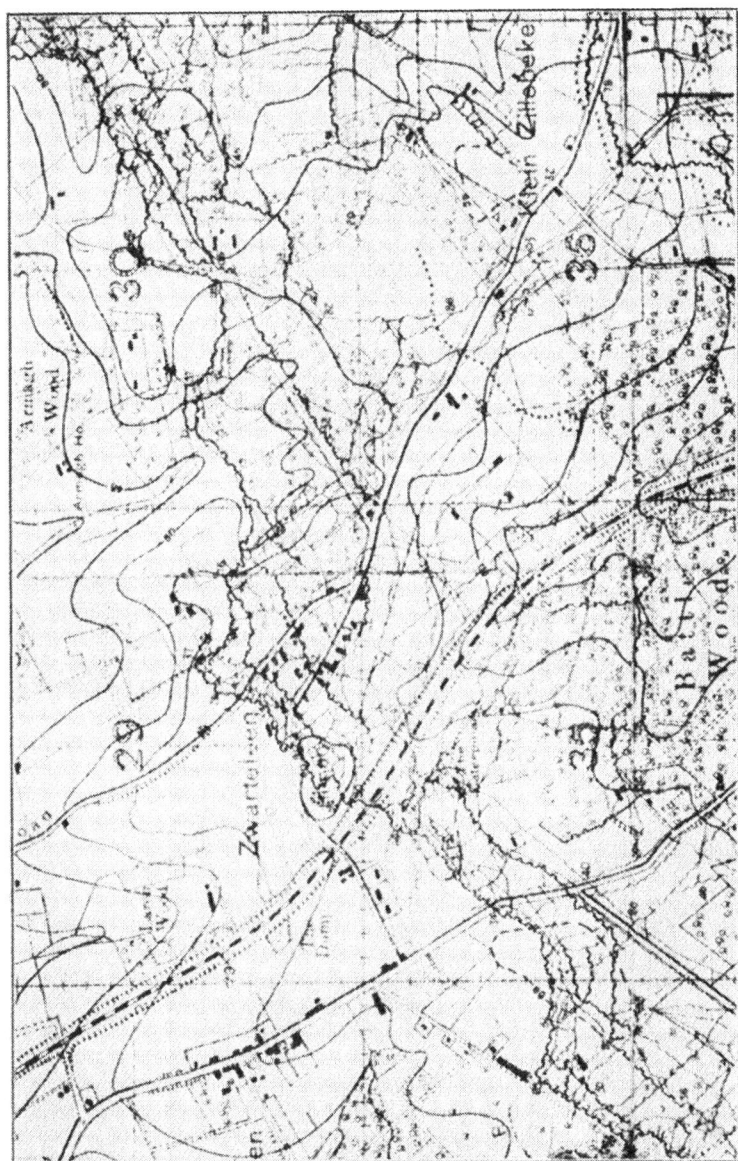

way, just a week later, I noticed that a big shell had gone through our carefully prepared "bomb-proof" and completely wrecked it. We only remained a few days and then received orders to go into the front line at Hill 60 (south of Hooge), as an attack was to be made to recover the trenches lost on the second.

As we had never been in the sector it was necessary for the non-commissioned officers to go in a day ahead to locate the gun positions and be able to guide the section in. We went in in daylight (the non-coms.) and found it to be the longest trip we had ever undertaken on such a mission. From Bedford House, on the reserve line, it is at least two miles to the front line, all the way exposed to observation and fire. There had been a little trench tramway but it had been wrecked by shells. By breaking our party up into twos we escaped any severe shelling and the rifle fire was at such long range that we ignored it. Beyond three hundred yards the German's shooting is a joke.

We went over the position which extends from

what was known as the Ravine, to a point exactly opposite Hill 60. At some places the lines were less than forty yards apart and it was possible to throw hand grenades back and forth. It required the entire day to familiarize ourselves with the wonderful maze of communication and support trenches at this place, as we had never seen anything like it before. We had become so accustomed to doing without communication trenches that they were a distinct novelty. They, together with the many support trenches, made a perfect labyrinth: like a spider's web, only not quite so regular in form.

The next night we moved in. As the battalion was crossing the long open stretch we came under fire from an enemy machine gun and some men were hit. There's no use talking, no other weapon used in the war is as deadly as a machine gun. Where you can walk through an artillery barrage with a few casualties, the well-directed fire of only one machine gun will pile men up as fast as they come along. When one of them catches you in the open the only thing to do is to drop into the nearest hole and stay there until the firing ceases.

We went in on the night of the twelfth and the attack was scheduled for the night of the thirteenth, or rather the morning of the fourteenth, as the preliminary bombardment was to commence at twelve-forty-five and "zero" was one-thirty A. M.

This was the greatest place I have ever seen for rifle grenades and "Minnies." They came over in flocks or shoals and one must be everlastingly on the lookout to dodge them. But we had as many as they and also a lot of Stokes guns which seemed to "put the fear of God" into the boche. They sprung a new "Minnie" here, much larger than any we had seen. It hurled a whale of a shell; not less than one hundred and sixty pounds of pure T. N. T., and what it did to our trenches and dug-outs was a sin. And the worst of it was, they had it in a hole in a deep railroad cutting at the bottom of Hill 60, where our artillery could not reach it.

At this time we had both the regular machine

guns and also a lot of Lewis automatic rifles. Shortly after, the latter were turned over to the infantry companies, while the former were taken into the newly-organized machine gun corps, an entirely separate branch of the service, which was under the direct command of the Brigade Commander. The guns were distributed along the line in favorable locations for either defense or offense but, as there were no prepared emplacements, the men had but little protection.

Here our work, as at St. Eloi, was to support the advance; in fact, that is the normal function of machine guns in an attack, although the lighter automatic rifles of the Lewis type are usually with the assaulting troops.

Our "Higher Command" had learned a lesson from the St. Eloi experience and had brought up many new batteries, including a fair sprinkling of the "super-heavies" of twelve and fifteen-inch calibers. It has been said, on good authority, that we had more than one thousand guns concentrated on about a thousand yards of trench, or a gun to every yard, and I am perfectly willing to believe it after hearing them all at work. It was our first experience of that delightful situation where we had "superiority of fire" and it made everybody happy. Afterward, on the Somme and Ancre, it had become a permanent condition; but to us, who had been "carrying on" under the overwhelming odds of the German guns, it was a welcome change. It did our hearts good to hear those monster thirteen hundred and fifty pound "babies" coming over our heads with a "woosh" and landing in the lines across the way, on Hill 60, where they left marks like mine craters. We could put up with quite a lot just to see that, and although we were suffering considerably from the rifle grenades and the "Minnies," every one appeared to be in a good humor.

With everything ready we waited for the "zero" hour. Exactly at the designated time the artillery opened. It was as though all the hounds of hell were let loose. Such a wailing and screeching and hissing as filled the air, from the eighteen-pounders ("whizz-bangs"), which seemed to just shave our own parapet, to the gigantic missiles from the "How-guns," as the Howitzers are affectionately called, each with its own peculiar noise. The explosions became merged into a continual roaring crash, without pause or break. Then our Stokes guns joined in, and, if there ever was an infernal machine, that is it. Vomiting out shells as fast as they can be fed into its hungry maw; so fast, indeed, that it is possible for seven of them to be in the air at one time, from one gun, at a range of less than four hundred yards, it is the last word in rapid-fire artillery.

Of course the Emma Gees started at the head of the procession and kept up a continuous fire.

Fritz soon began to do the best he could but, what with the noise of our own guns and the bursting shells, we were unable to hear his unless they struck very close. He did give us trouble, though, with that devilish Minenwerfer which sent over a wheel-barrow load of high explosive at each shot. He blew the left end of our line "off the map" for a distance of a hundred yards or more and made it untenable—for any one but a machine gunner. The infantry was ordered to evacuate that part and did so, but not the Emma Gees; they stuck until one of the big "terrors," striking alongside, killed and wounded all the crew but one and then he still stuck it, loading and firing until I was able to get a reserve crew up to relieve him. He was a Scot, one of the kind that doesn't know what it means to quit. Here's to you, "Wullie" Shepherd, wherever you are!

The attack was carried off with absolute precision. At one-thirty the barrage lifted and over the boys went, sweeping everything before them, back to the original position and then a little farther for good measure. By daylight they had the new line so well consolidated that Fritz was never able to make a dent in it and the Canadian prestige was once more established.

At the left end of our line, where the Minenwerfer had done so much damage, was a mine shaft; one of many in that vicinity which our engineers were driving under Hill 60 (they

afterward blew it up), and it seemed as though
the boche knew of it and was endeavoring to cave
it in with the "Minnies." In fact, they did succeed
in partly destroying it, but the sheltering roof
at the mouth of the shaft remained in fair
condition, and as it was the only protective
covering in that neighborhood, Bouchard and
I were sitting inside, with our feet hanging down the shaft, holding down that end of the
line. We had relieved the other crew, or rather I
had sent them back about two hundred yards along
the trench as a precautionary measure and then,
feeling that some one *must* remain to keep lookout,
decided to take care of the job myself. The
boy, of course, insisted upon staying with me.
The big fellows were coming over with regular-
ity (I nearly said monotonous, but those things
never get monotonous), and were bursting too
close for comfort. Bou had just made a proposition that we sneak over after dark and try to
locate the devil-machine and blow it up, when we
heard something moving below us in the mine-
shaft, and a moment later a mud-encrusted face

Lewis Machine Gun Squad Observing with Periscope at Hill 60

came up into the light. With an unusually fluent flow of "language," which sounded strangely familiar to me, two men came up the ladder, and as the first one emerged into the daylight he took a look at me and said: "Hello, Mac; it's a long way to Ft. George, isn't it?" When he had removed some of the dirt from his face I recognized a miner, named McLeod, who had once helped rescue me from the Giscome Rapids and afterward worked for me up in British Columbia. He and his partner had been caught in the shaft and had been a day digging themselves out. After a rest of a few minutes they went their way, down the trench, and I never saw or heard of them again.

During the next hour or two I managed to work around through the wreckage of this part of our line, searching for wounded and making a list of the dead. I found none of the former, all having been removed by their companions when they were ordered to evacuate, but I did find a number of bodies which I examined for identification disks or other marks and made a complete record which I afterward turned in to our Headquarters. This is a custom that is always followed, if possible, so that, in the event that your own troops do not return to that spot, a record will be preserved and relatives notified. If this were not done, many would be reported as "missing" which is, to relatives, far more terrible than the knowledge that death has been swift and sure. This is work in which many chaplains have especially distinguished themselves, often working close behind the advancing lines during a battle; writing last messages for the dying and compiling lists of the dead who may or may not be buried at a later date.

In burying dead on the field, every effort is made so to mark the grave that it may afterward be identified and a proper record obtained for the archives of the Graves Registration Commission. The best way is to write all the data, name, regiment and number together with the date, on a piece of paper, place it in a bottle and stick the bottle, neck down, in the top of the grave. If no bottle is available, the next best way is to write the record on a smooth piece of wood with an ordinary lead pencil which will withstand the action of water far better than ink or indelible pencil.

Here I had my last talk with Bouchard. He was very anxious to go to college and take an engineering course. I suggested Purdue, but he thought he would find it necessary to spend a year or two at some preparatory school. He had heard me speak of Culver and was very much interested in that place, and when I left it was definitely decided that, should he survive the war, he would spend at least four years at any educational institution I might recommend.

As soon as darkness came our infantry returned, and by working hard all night managed to restore the damaged part of the parapet. I went back to my dug-out for a little sleep and had just made myself comfortable when a six-inch shell struck the place and drove me out, together with a companion, George Paudash, a Chippeway Indian and corporal of our section. We had several Indians, there being two pairs of brothers, all from the same reservation and all of them splendid soldiers.

We had several men hit that night by rifle grenades. I particularly remember two: Flanagan and McFarland. The former was hit in numerous places, some of them really serious, but was most concerned over a little scratch on his face which he was afraid would injure his good-looks. McFarland, just a boy, about eighteen, had his left hand terribly mangled and nearly twenty pieces of metal in other parts of his body, but he laughed and called out: "I've got my Blighty; I've got my Blighty." His brother had been shot through both eyes and totally blinded a short time before. By the merest chance I saw McFarland a few days later, as he was being taken aboard a hospital ship at Boulogne and he then gave me his wrist watch, which had been shattered and driven into the flesh, asking that I send it to his father in Canada. I sent it by registered post, from London, but never heard from it.

The artillery fighting continued for several days and on the night of the eighteenth we were relieved and moved back to Bedford House, in reserve.

Next morning I was summoned to Battalion Headquarters and informed that I had been commissioned and was ordered back to England to act as an instructor in one of the training divisions. Our Colonel at this time also received his promotion to Brigadier-General and he promised, as soon as he was assigned to a brigade, that he would request I be transferred to his command as brigade machine gun officer. He did, afterward, make an effort to have this done, but it was too late. I had finally got my "long Blighty," and was out.

It was hard to part from that old crowd. I did not know when I would get back, but we all knew, without question, that there would be other faces gone from the ranks before we met again. When I did return, during the Somme campaign, I was attached to another battalion and did not often see the Twenty-first and when I did, I recognized but few of them. They had taken part in the great advance of September fifteenth, which captured Courcellette and numerous other towns—the greatest gain ever made in one day on the Western Front until the recent one at Cambrai—and had helped to add another glorious page to Canada's brilliant record. But the cost was great. Many, oh, so many of the bravest and the best fell that day and among them was "my little boy," Bouchard, killed at the age of eighteen, after two years of service.

Yes; a boy in years, but he worked like a man, fought like a man and, thank God, he died like a man—out in front, fighting.

CHAPTER XVII

Down an Out—for a While

WHILE the following has no direct connection with the machine guns, and is, really, a part of "another story," I think it fitting that I take this opportunity to render my humble tribute of gratitude and admiration for the splendid work of the British Red Cross Society; and that the reader may fully understand, it is necessary to relate the occurrences which led up to my first hospital experience.

Upon returning to England, I was assigned to a Training Battalion at our old camp—Sandling—but found the work so tedious and monotonous that I requested a transfer to other and more active duties, and soon after was engaged first, in conducting troops to France; then, as a messenger to and from the various headquarters; later, on court-martial work at Rouen and Le Havre; and finally reassigned to the Fourth

THE EMMA GEES

Canadian Brigade and ordered to the front, during the latter part of the Somme Battle. I was with a party of officers of the Gloucestershire and the "Ox and Bucks" (Oxford and Buckinghamshire) Regiments and through an error on the part of the R. T. O. (railway transportation officer) my transportation order was made out the same as theirs, and the first thing I knew I was away over on the right of our line, opposite Combles, where we joined the French. As there was a fight on, I went in with the "Glosters," and after the fall of Combles made my way up the line until I located my own command, near Courcellette.

Here I heard of the great advance of September fifteenth and also of the death of many of my old friends. Among them, it seemed, Bouchard and his crew had been wiped out by a big shell, but no one had been able to get back to look for them or bury them. I was very busy, but getting all available information as to the spot where they were seen to fall, I managed, at night, to make several trips over the ground, but without result.

DOWN AND OUT—FOR A WHILE

The spot was near the famous "Sugar Refinery," just outside the village, and as this had been one of the hottest places in the fight, there were many bodies lying around but none that I could recognize.

I had a cross made, bearing the names of all the crew and decided that, at the first opportunity, I would plant it at that spot; and when our whole division was ordered out, on October tenth, I took the cross and made my way up the Bapaume road and across the shell-torn field to the place. The enemy was shelling the road, dropping several heavies near me, so I hastily gathered into a shell-hole the remains of all the dead in the immediate vicinity and covered them up as best I could, then placed the cross firmly in the ground and turned to leave. I had not gone far when a "crump" struck so close as to stun and partly bury me. When I regained my senses I found that I could not see. My eyes, especially the left, had been giving me a great deal of trouble ever since I had been hit on the side of the face by a piece of shell at the time of the Bluff fight, but now they appeared to be entirely out of commission, and were very painful.

I lay there for some time, trying to figure some way out of it, all the time hearing the shells coming over. This gave me an idea. Knowing the direction from which the shells came with relation to the location of the road, I started out to make my way there. Troops were continually passing at night and I would be sure to find assistance.

From that time on my remembrance of things is not clear. I have hazy recollections of falling into a trench, crawling out and getting tangled up in some wire and then, I think I fell into another hole. I do remember, distinctly, talking aloud to myself, as though to another person, and telling him to "get down on your knees and crawl, you damn fool: first thing you know you'll fall into one of those deep holes and break your neck."

Whatever I did after that must have been done instinctively. (Was afterward told that I was found, lying stretched out across the Bapaume road.)

N. N. MONT-S'-ELOI P.-de-C. — GUERRE 1914-1916 — En
face de la rue des Tours, on évacue un Allemand blessé;
les nôtres sont pleins d'attention pour lui adoucir ses
souffrances. Quel contraste avec leurs procédés!...

Removing the German Wounded from Mont St. Eloi

DOWN AND OUT—FOR A WHILE

The next thing I knew I suddenly discovered that I was trying to *think* of something. I believe I was conscious. I felt as though I *could* move if I wanted to, but didn't want to. I could see nothing, but that also was of no importance. It was something else that was wrong and it worried me in a vague, half-interested sort of way. One thing was sure—I was dead, all right, and it wasn't half bad. Even if I couldn't see or move or think, I was not suffering any pain or inconvenience, which was a great relief from "soldiering." Nothing seemed to matter, anyway, and I guess I went to sleep.

I felt, or rather sensed, the presence of others moving about from time to time, but took no interest in the matter until, suddenly, back came the old feeling that something was not right— that there had been a big change in all the affairs of the world—and then, after what seemed hours of struggling with the problem, it came to me like a flash—it was the "quiet" that was bothering me. That was it; there was no noise; and then, my brain becoming clearer all the time, I began to wonder whether I was deaf or whether the war was over. It occurred to me that I might clap my hands or make some movement to find out whether or not I could hear, but the idea was dismissed as involving too much exertion; just as it was too much work to open my eyes to try to see.

Then I *heard* some one come close to me, heard voices, faint and far away they seemed, so I shouted to them (I thought I shouted but it was only a mumbling whisper), and then a voice, low and close at hand, asked me: "Are you awake?"

"Course; what's matter?"

"Nothing is the matter; you're all right now. Don't you think you could eat something?"

I pondered that for some time, but as I was quite comfortable and could not see the sense of dead folks eating, anyhow, I declined and fell asleep again. It was too much trouble to talk, especially to answer questions.

When next I awoke it was different. I actually opened my eyes, or at least one of them, the other being bandaged, and I could see a face

DOWN AND OUT—FOR A WHILE

looking down at me—a face and a white expanse
of something with a brilliant red cross in the
center, and when the face asked me how I felt
now and did I think I could eat a little,
I grunted something which was intended
to assure her that I was feeling all right and
was hungry. At any rate, she understood, and
disappearing, soon returned with a tray, loaded
with things. She first helped me hold up my head
while she gave me a tumblerful of hot milk with
brandy in it, but that was no good—it would not
stay down; so, after a little trouble on that ac-
count, she vanished again and came back with
a pint bottle of champagne which she opened and
fed to me; first a spoonful at a time and then a
full glass. That paved the way all right and I
was able to eat something, I don't remember
just what, but it was good.

By this time I had discovered that I still had
all my hands and feet and could move them about.
Satisfied on that point, I asked where I was.

"Hospital; but you mustn't talk."

"What hospital; why can't I talk?"

"Number Twelve; but I think you should keep quiet and rest."

"Had plenty rest; where's Number Twelve?"

"St. Pol; but, really, you must go to sleep now."

I went to sleep, wondering how the dickens I happened to be in St. Paul, which was what I understood her to say. (The French spell it differently but pronounce it about the same.)

From that time on, scarcely an hour passed that one of the kindly nurses or sisters did not come in and look to see if I was awake, and if so, could they get me something to eat or drink. It was heaven, all right; or at least, my idea of what heaven should be.

I learned that, although I was disabled on the night of the tenth, I was not picked up until the twelfth and then had been relayed through several dressing stations and hospitals until I landed in Number Twelve General Hospital, at the town of St. Pol. It was a B. R. C. (British Red Cross) institution and was altogether different from my preconceived ideas of hospitals. The day when I first "woke up" was the fifteenth of October, my birthday.

After several days I was put aboard a hospital train and taken to LeTreport, where I was assigned to Lady Murray's Hospital, another B. R. C. place. It had been, before the war, The Golf Hotel, one of the many splendid seaside hotels that have been converted into hospitals. Here, again, I was royally treated. Every wish appeared to be anticipated by the indefatigable and ever-cheerful women and girls, many of them volunteers, members of prominent and even titled families. Lady Murray personally visited every patient at least once a day.

All these ambulances at LeTreport are driven by girls belonging to the V. A. D. I'm not sure whether it means Volunteer Ambulance Department or Volunteer Aïd Department, but that is immaterial; they are wonders, whatever name they sail under.

They work all hours, day or night, transferring patients to and from trains and hospitals.

THE EMMA GEES

They furnished their own uniforms and paid all their own expenses, and for a long time served without any compensation, but I have heard that a small allowance has been made them recently.

The girl who took us down to the train told me that she had been over there two years. I asked her if it was not pretty hard work and she replied: "Oh, sometimes it is hard, when the weather is bad, but we know it is nothing to what the men are doing up in front, so we are glad to be able to do our little bit, wherever we can."

Going down the hill, we passed a big ambulance, filled with wounded, standing alongside the road. A little slip of a girl, who looked as though she weighed about ninety pounds, was changing a tire and I honestly believe that that tire and rim weighed as much as she did. Our driver stopped and proffered assistance but the little one declined, remarking that we'd better hurry or she would beat us to the train. As a matter of fact, she was not five minutes after us.

I was in pretty bad shape; could see very little and had an attack of trench fever. As soon as I was able to travel I was sent, with several others, by hospital train to Le Havre, where we went aboard the hospital ship *Carisbrook Castle,* landing at Southampton, and so on to London, where I was lucky enough to draw an assignment to another B. R. C. hospital—Mrs. Pollock's, at 50 Weymouth Street. And here I remained until, passed on by numerous "boards" and subjected to many examinations, I found myself again on the way to France, where I reported the fifth of December—still able to "carry on."

Herbert W. McBride
1873 - 1933

by Jack McPherson

Herbert McBride's two military books, The Emma Gees and A Rifleman Went to War, touch only lightly on his biography. We thought it appropriate to add some additional information on his life. We would like to thank the Indiana State Library, the National Archives of Canada, Michel Perrier and Ron Zemancik for their assistance.

Herbert Wes McBride was born October 15, 1873 in Waterloo, Indiana, to Robert W. and Ida S. Chamberlain McBride. The family had a tradition of military service. McBride's grandfather was killed in the Mexican War, and his father served in the Union cavalry during the Civil War. His father also enjoyed a distinguished legal career, ultimately becoming a judge on the Indiana Supreme Court.

Little information on McBride's youth is available. His passions seem to have been military service and small arms. The attestation papers he filled out for the Canadian Army in 1915 indicate his occupation was lawyer, but he seems to have spent most of his early years in the North. He was in the Klondike gold rush of 1897 and also worked in railroad construction in British Columbia. He was heavily involved with the Indiana National Guard during the pre-World War One years and by 1915 had logged over 21 years of service. He advanced to the rank of captain and, in addition to his command duties, coached a highly successful rifle team in the Guard.

Mcbride's service in the Canadian Expeditionary Force would ultimately prove what he doubtless anticipated, the pivotal event in his life. Coming from a family where his male forebears had served in America's wars for decades (he was also a Son of the American Revolution), the reluctance of American politicians to become involved in The Great War was a source of personal frustration to McBride. Combined with his thwarted attempt to join the British forces in the Boer War and his obvious desire to put his specialized military skills to use, his early enlistment in one of the Allied armies should have come as no surprise.

Although McBride amply chronicles the more significant events of his Canadian service, there is little information in his books on his actual assignments. The following chronology appeared in the Indiana Book of Merit, a tribute to Indianans who distinguished themselves in World War One (McBride is flanked in the book by an Army Sergeant who won the DSC and a Private with the Silver Star). "Entered service February 1, 1915, Ottawa, Canada. Captain, 38th Battalion, Canadian Army, February 1, 1915. Resigned March 19, 1915. Enlisted, Canadian Army, April 3, 1915, Kingston, Ont. Training: Kingston and Barriefield, Canada; West Sandling Camp, Kent, England. Assigned to 21st Battalion, Canadian Expeditionary Force; transferred to Headquarters Staff, 2d Canadian Division; to 21st Battalion, C.E.F.; to 39th Reserve Battalion; to 18th Battalion. Sergeant, December 26, 1915; Lieutenant (temporary), May 31, 1916. Overseas May 20, 1915 - April 15, 1917. Battles: St. Eloi Craters, Le Havre, Rouen, Somme, Thiepval Ridge, Ancre Heights (Regina Trench). Discharged November 9, 1916."

This information was probably reconstructed from his memory and does contain errors (i.e., date of discharge precedes last date of overseas service) but gives a general feel for McBride's C.E.F. assignments. It also mentions his citation for the British Military Medal, awarded in June of 1916. Not everything is shown here, however. McBride's modesty likely caused him not to mention the seven wounds he received or his two medals from the French. His discretion kept him from revealing one or two other facts.

Despite his many years of peacetime service with the Guard, McBride was apparently no garrison soldier. A terror on the battlefield, he seems to have followed the warrior tradition of being in scrapes "off-duty". Following his return from overseas, one incident resulted in a court martial and separation from the Canadian service. A confidential letter (date and author illegible) describes the occasion, "At noon on Wednesday the 17th instant, Captain H.W. McBride, dressed in uniform and wearing a Stetson hat, became intoxicated (where, I do not know). Later in the afternoon, he procured a horse, and for the better part of an hour, gave an exhibition of his qualities in horse-man-ship (sic) on the main street of Ottawa (Sparks St.), and at one time, was performing for about two hundred people in front of the Russell Hotel, at the same time telling them who he was, what he was, and what he came to Canada for. He afterwards rode to the Officer's Mess, corner Lyon and Queen Streets, and tying his horse to the side verandah, entered. Two officers endeavoured to keep him, but he would not remain and left a few minutes later taking his horse with him." The reaction of officers cut in the old British mold to such an escapade can be imagined. Canadian Army records show him being dismissed in February of 1917. He apparently spent the next few months instructing at Culver Military Academy.

With the entry of the United States into the war in 1917, there was more work for McBride to do. Reentering the Indiana Guard as a captain in August of 1917, his first assignment was to the 139th Machine Gun Battalion, 38th Division, as an instructor. He subsequently served out the war at Camp Perry, teaching marksmanship and sniping. It was about this time that he wrote The Emma Gees, and the memories of his combat service in France must have been quite fresh. He resigned from the Army in October 1918 and spent several years after the war in the lumber business around Portland, Oregon.

Much of the five years preceding McBride's death was spent in compiling his masterwork, A Rifleman Went to War, which was published posthumously in 1935. Mary E. Bostwick, reviewing the book in the Indianapolis Star, was prescient in writing (January 19, 1936), "Nearly three years after his death a monument, better than any marble shaft, has been raised to the memory of Capt. Herbert W. McBride, conceded by many military men to be Indiana's most distinguished soldier, who was as well a world traveler and author and a marksman whose proficiency with the rifle and machine gun amounted to genius. It is his own book, A Rifleman Went to War...".

Herbert McBride died at his home in Indianapolis on March 17, 1933. He is buried in Crown Hill Cemetery in the McBride family plot, a plot marked by a large granite stone bearing the family name. But truly as Mary Bostwick wrote in 1936, his words are his greatest monument. As the twentieth century draws to a close, McBride's observations on the use of small arms in battle still stand as definitive. There are few people seriously interested in the tactical use of firearms who do not have McBride's writings on their shelves. America's most highly respected military, law enforcement and clandestine organizations continue to look to him as an authority. If and when Americans must again go into battle, their ranks will include men who have spent long hours on the practice ranges and have read their McBride. These are the men the enemy will least want to encounter - and that would please Herbert McBride very much.

www.ingramcontent.com/pod-product-compliance
Lightning Source LLC
Chambersburg PA
CBHW031600110426

42742CB00036B/261